Praise For

Redefining Racism: How Racism Became "Power + Prejudice"

"For anyone genuinely committed to realizing an American future where race, racism, and 'anti-racism,' cease to be the tools used to divide us, this is an indispensable text. With *Redefining Racism*, Jake Klein has provided a national service."

> — Thomas Chatterton Williams, fellow at the American Enterprise Institute, author of *Self-Portrait in Black and White* & *Losing My Cool*

"Adherents of 'anti-racism' have committed mass-revisions of the words we rely upon to convey meaning ('racism,' 'blackness,' 'race,') and then moralized their incorrect use. Klein traces the evolution of these terms, illuminating how and why activists have hoodwinked society. *Redefining Racism* is a must-read for anyone engaged in today's debates on race and equality—or simply desiring a return to sanity."

> — Peter Boghossian, fellow at the University of Austin, author of *How to Have Impossible Conversations* & *A Manual for Creating Atheists*

"Jake has written a compelling, urgent, and courageous book that goes to places many shy away from. To say everyone on the planet needs to read it is an understatement, but I'll say it anyway!"

> — Africa Brooke, author of *The Third Perspective*

"*Redefining Racism* takes a deep dive into the origins of modern 'anti-racism' and exposes a troubling legacy of recycled ideas and dangerous tactics. Through meticulous research, Klein traces these ideas to a group whose methods shaped not only today's Diversity, Equity, and Inclusion landscape but also left psychological casualties in their wake. A must-read for anyone seeking to understand the dangerous undercurrents of today's DEI industry."

— Colin Wright, fellow at the Manhattan Institute,
Founding Editor of Reality's Last Stand

"Modern vernacular has been infected with alternate definitions for terms that stem from insidious Marxist origins, especially for the word 'racism.' In the fascinating and engaging *Redefining Racism*, Jake Klein takes readers on a thorough yet disturbing ride through American history to pinpoint where the 'Power + Prejudice' definition started and how it spread into today's popular culture. Klein's vital research illustrates how our failure to adequately understand the past allows for bad ideas to be resurrected as supposed new concepts for public consumption."

— Adam B. Coleman, author of *Black Victim to
Black Victor*

"*Redefining Racism* is a solid piece of historiography, enriching historical understanding—social, intellectual, and institutional. The study is honestly undertaken, carefully reasoned, and temperately written."

— Daniel B. Klein, professor of economics at George
Mason Univerity, author of *Smithian Morals* &
Knowledge and Coordination

Redefining Racism

How Racism Became "Power + Prejudice"

Joseph (Jake) Klein

Black
Sheep
Books

Cover design by Christina Berry

Published by Black Sheep Books

The Black Sheep
14120A Route 29
P.O. Box #21
Centreville, VA 20122
WeTheBlackSheep.com

First Edition: September 2024

Library of Congress Control Number: 2024914840

ISBNs: 979-8-218-00095-0 (paperback), 979-8-218-00094-3 (e-book)

Contents

Introduction

On June 10, 2020, the New York Times and numerous other publications reported that Merriam-Webster's dictionary would officially change its definition of "racism." Up until this point, the dictionary had included three definitions: "a belief that race is the primary determinant of human traits and capacities and that racial differences produce an inherent superiority of a particular race," "a doctrine or political program based on the assumption of racism and designed to execute its principles/a political or social system founded on racism," and perhaps most regular in common parlance, "racial prejudice or discrimination."

Merriam-Webster changed their definition after receiving an email from 22-year-old recent college graduate Kennedy Mitchum. As a student, Mitchum had been frustrated that in discussions with other students about racism, her definition would often be challenged with the dictionary cited as evidence against her, and people she accused of being racist would deny it by appealing to that same definition. "Racism is not only prejudice against a certain race due to the color of a person's skin, as it states in your dictionary,"

Mitchum wrote to Merriam-Webster, "it is both prejudice combined with social and institutional power."[1]

The job of a dictionary is not to decide how language should be used but rather to record how it is used in practice. This is an important function to aid in human communication. For better or worse, as anyone discussing racism in modern times has noticed, "Power + Prejudice" and similar definitions have become increasingly common.

This book is the story of how that happened.

The "Power + Prejudice" definition was coined and spread in the context of what was then called "Racism Awareness Training"— now often referred to as "diversity training" or by similar names. Thus, the story of the coining of "Power + Prejudice" is also the story of Racism Awareness Training and its wider philosophy of race. As protests in response to the killing of George Floyd raised the public conversation around racism to levels unseen in decades, and as Merriam-Webster was making the decision to update their definition, Robin DiAngelo's *White Fragility* hit #1 on the New York Times bestseller's list, having been on the list since its debut two years prior.[2] DiAngelo is perhaps the world's most well-known Racism Awareness Training teacher; her book is a distillation and update of the same philosophy that has been spread through Racism Awareness Training since its origin.

Thus, this story is also a history of the origins of *White Fragility* and DiAngelo's worldview.

That worldview can be traced as far back as pre-history. Human evolution has predisposed us to a type of moral thinking adaptive for small groups of individuals that the birth of civilization has long

---

1. Hauser, "Merriam-Webster Revises 'Racism' Entry After Missouri Woman Asks for Changes."
2. New York Times, "The New York Times Best Sellers."

since moved us away from.[3] Since then various intellectual currents have developed upon these moral impulses, including but not limited to certain religious movements and political movements such as Marxism. In the interest of telling a contained story this book starts in the year 1967—a pivotal year for the development of Racism Awareness Training—but it should not be seen as *creatio ex nihilo*.

According to a June 2020 YouGov poll, shortly after the death of Floyd, only 30 percent of US adults thought that "race relations in the United States are generally good"; 70 percent thought the converse.[4] 16.8 percent of Americans admitted to holding an unfavorable impression of blacks, 13.7 percent an unfavorable impression of Latinos, 13.4 percent an unfavorable impression of Asians, and 18.2 percent an unfavorable impression of whites.[5] That such views could be so widespread is an unacceptable state of affairs. The question at hand is not *whether* fighting racism is important, but *how* can we do so effectively? And more specifically, are the currently dominant "anti-racism" strategies helping or making things worse?

I hope to reveal in this book that the "Power + Prejudice" definition of racism, and its associated ideas spread via Racism Awareness Training, are making things *much* worse. I recognize that this book is certain to be controversial. It refutes a definition of racism that has become orthodoxy to much of the anti-racist movement; simply disagreeing with it can get you labeled a racist.[6]

---

3. For more see Hayek, "The Atavism of Social Justice."
4. Frankovic, "Optimism Grows Among Black Americans That Protests Will Improve How Police Treat Them."
5. Sidney, "There's a Huge Gap in How Republicans and Democrats See Discrimination."
6. Why that is and the thinker that caused this be will be a focus of Part 2 of this book.

The "Power + Prejudice" definition is often used to argue that black people in America cannot be racist against whites because black people lack institutional power. This famously occurred in the defense of then newly-hired New York Times editorial board member Sarah Jeong after her anti-white tweets sparked conservative outrage.[7] In my own personal experience, I have been told that pushing back on this definition demonstrates that my motive is to defend "white people" or the "powerful."

Thus, I want to clearly state my purpose: Regardless of how others would define me, I see myself as a committed anti-racist, and I believe that racism in America still affects black Americans and other minority Americans significantly more than white Americans. My interest is not in defending white people, but in the complete integration of all Americans. I want to bring about a future where race is not used to divide us, where no one is ever discriminated against or viewed with prejudice due to the color of their skin. I believe this is achievable, but this will only be possible if our society comes to a genuine agreement that such prejudice and discrimination is indeed evil. This will benefit all of us—white, black, or any other color—but it will likely help no group more than black Americans.

If you are going into reading this with the desire to refute it, I implore you to instead read it with an open mind. Please understand that, like you, I am genuinely trying to find the best path to a world where racism is a concern of the past, and struggling persons of any race can have a better life. To those who would say a white person has no business professing expertise on what racism is or isn't, I would alert you that all the major figures responsible for creating

---

7.   Camp, "Democratic Strategist Claims Sarah Jeong Tweets Aren't Racist Because Racism Is 'Prejudice Plus Power.'"

and forwarding the "Power + Prejudice" definition were white and felt the need to work on the subject explicitly due to their whiteness.

I believe that the views and tactics of the far-Left on this subject, which in recent times have bled heavily into the mainstream, have set our society back by at least a generation in ending racism. That is certainly not their intent; most of the individuals discussed in this book believed that their work would help to oppose racism. Nonetheless, I believe our country's regression on race is the result of their mistaken views. If we do not correct society's view of what racism is, we may forever lose the possibility to end racism and fulfill Martin Luther King Jr.'s dream.

Part One

The Origins of "Power + Prejudice" & Racism Awareness Training

The Long, Hot Summer of 1967

The first use of "Power + Prejudice" in cited writing is a simple bullet point on a list of definitions of racism, with no explanation of where it came from or why it was a proper definition.[1] Contrary to the appeals to authority of many "anti-racist" activists today, this definition was not proposed by a sociologist or an academic race theorist, but rather a high school educator in Wayne County, Michigan.[2] In 1970, Patricia Ann Fitzsimmons Bidol (a.k.a. Pat Bidol and later Patricia Bidol-Padva) authored *Developing New Perspectives on Race: An Innovative Multi-Media Social Studies Curriculum in Race Relations for the Secondary Level* intended to teach high school students to be "anti-racists."

To understand why Bidol invented this new definition for her

---

1. Bidol, *Developing New Perspectives on Race*, 34–35.
2. See this example, watched by hundreds of thousands of people, of an appeal to authority from MTV News, crediting the definition to sociologists. Ramsey, "5 Things Everyone Should Know About Racism."

curriculum, one must first look back three years earlier, to the "long, hot summer of 1967."

2) Racism

   a) According to Random House Dictionary of the English Language, 1967:

      (1) A belief that human races have distinctive characteristics that determine their respective cultures, usually involving the idea that one's own race is superior and has the right to rule others.

      (2) A policy of enforcing such assorted rights.

      (3) A system of government and society based upon it.

   b) Perpetuation of belief in the superiority of the white race.

   c) Power + Prejudice.

   d) Any activity by individuals, groups, institutions, or cultures that treats human beings unjustly because of color and rationalizes that treatment by attributing to them undesirable biological, psychological, social, or cultural characteristics. (Robert Terry, For Whites Only)

   e) Far from being the simple delusion of a bigoted and ignorant minority, racism is a set of beliefs whose structure arises from the deepest levels of our lives --from the fabric of assumptions we make about the world, ourselves, and others, and from the patterns of our fundamental social activities. (Dr. Joel Kovel, White Racism: A Psycho-History)

The first appearance of "Power + Prejudice" on record.

During what has become known as the "long, hot summer of

1967," 159 race riots occurred across the United States, leading to at least 85 deaths, 2,100 injuries, and 11,000 arrests.[3] About half of those deaths occurred at the summer's biggest riot in Detroit.[4]

On July 23, 1967, a Detroit Police Department officer raided an unlicensed drinking club (known as a "blind pig") in the office of the United Community League for Civic Action, a civil rights organization. Despite the fact that the 82 people inside were celebrating the return of local GIs from Vietnam, the police chose to arrest all present. A crowd of onlookers witnessed this abuse of police power and the club's doorman, William Walter Scott III, threw a bottle at a police officer, initiating a riot.

As soon as the police left, looting began, quickly expanding to the whole neighborhood. As the riot reached critical mass, Mayor Jerome Cavanagh enacted a curfew, but that did little to stop the violence that had already overwhelmed city police. The next day, state police were called to Detroit to assist, and Governor George Romney requested federal assistance for a crisis that had gotten so out of control that state troopers and police officers were simply making as many arrests as they could, without discriminating between civilians and criminals. The district's congressman, John Conyers, then in his first term, attempted to ease tensions by driving with a loudspeaker and asking people to go home; his car was pelted with rocks and bottles instead. By the end of the day, 483 fires had been lit, 231 incidents were reported each hour, over 2,500 guns were looted from local stores, and 1,800 people were arrested.

On the third day, President Lyndon Johnson authorized the use of federal troops, sending in the Air Force and Army National Guard. Detroit police were found to have committed acts of abuse

---

3. Sidney, *"Rioters and Judges."*
    Fine, *Violence in the Model City*, 229.
4. Kresnak, *Hope for the City*, 15

against both black and white people who were in their custody, as well as women and others out past curfew. Though it took 48 more hours and the use of tanks and machine guns, by the fifth day the riot was brought under control. Approximately, 10,000 people had participated in the riots, 43 had died, and 7,200 had been arrested.

Before the riot had even ended, President Johnson appointed the National Advisory Commission on Civil Disorders, also known as the Kerner Commission (named after its chair, Illinois Governor Otto Kerner Jr.) with the goal of answering three questions: "What happened? Why did it happen? What can be done to prevent it from happening again and again?" Seven months later the commission produced its report, which instantly became a bestseller.

The commission stated, "this is our basic conclusion: our nation is moving toward two societies, one black, one white—separate and unequal" and "what white Americans have never fully understood—but what the Negro can never forget—is that white society is deeply implicated in the ghetto. White institutions created it, white institutions maintain it, and white society condones it," placing the bulk of the blame for the unrest that summer on the conditions in which white Americans had left black Americans. While white racism clearly played a large role in putting black Americans in poor conditions, particularly at that point in history, just after the civil rights movement, this focus was controversial. After all, if we accept that human beings possess the agency to be responsible for their actions, isn't it appropriate to put the primary blame on the rioters themselves? Looking back years later, Harvard University history professor Stephan Thernstrom would ask:

> Because the commission took for granted that the riots were the fault of white racism, it would have been awkward to have had to confront the question of why liberal Detroit blew up while Birmingham and other

Southern cities—where conditions for blacks were infinitely worse—did not. Likewise, if the problem was white racism, why didn't the riots occur in the 1930s, when prevailing white racial attitudes were far more barbaric than they were in the 1960s?[5]

Nevertheless, the commission's findings were well-considered and overwhelmingly accurate—although the solutions it suggested could be debated. But in less methodical hands, the notion that white society is the sole problem that needs fixing in America would prove quite dangerous. As a Racism Awareness Trainer would recall:

> The Kerner Commission was … important because it had the aura of legitimacy, so when you were talking about this theory in public and in your trainings and to people who would be resistant to this message, you could use the findings of the Kerner Commission as the authority to support your position. Whereas using the words of Malcolm X or other black activists wasn't going to get you anywhere in terms of … opening the door and asking people to think about these issues in terms of, 'What's your responsibility?' 'What's the white community's responsibility?' … Broaching that discussion, and not having people immediately shut off, the only way to open that door was to use the Kerner Commission.[6]

5.　Stur, "Kerner Commission Report."
6.　Burgin, "The Workshop as the Work." 134-135.

Detroit Responds to the Riots

The day the riot ended, Mayor Cavanagh and Governor Romney invited 160 community leaders to attend a meeting to consider Detroit's "current and future problems." The heads of Detroit's three major auto companies—General Motors, Ford, and Chrysler—were at the meeting and all on board. Chrysler's Lynn Townsend said, "we'd *better* make an extra effort. Detroit is the test tube for America. If the concentrated power of industry and government can't solve the problems of the ghetto *here*, God help our country." Cavanagh and Romney asked Joseph L. Hudson Jr., president of the company that operated Detroit's largest department store, to lead a committee to "coordinate the public and private resources necessary to help rebuild [Detroit's] social and physical fabric." That committee would be named the "New Detroit Committee" (and would later incorporate as New Detroit, Inc.), and would feature Hudson, Cavanagh, and Romney as its founding members.

To seek guidance in structuring his committee, Hudson turned to Hugo White and James Campbell, leaders of the Detroit

Industrial Mission (DIM): "a church related organization involved with the social impact of industrial development" that Hudson had been on the board of earlier that decade.[1] At the time, DIM was pursuing a strategy of working with militant black radicals, and it advised Hudson to do the same. White and Campbell believed the "ghetto community" had demonstrated its "power to tear Detroit apart" and that "the established Negro leadership" was out of touch with the black militant movement.[2]

White and Campbell arranged a meeting for black militants to advise Hudson on the operation of and membership in New Detroit. Milton Henry—vice president of the Republic of New Afrika, a black separatist movement that sought to create an ethno-state by claiming the territory of Louisiana, Mississippi, Alabama, Georgia, and South Carolina—agreed at the meeting that black nationalists should participate in the reconstruction of Detroit.[3] Albert B. Cleage Jr., leader of a local black nationalist church, denounced the NAACP and other mainstream black leadership organizations as "Uncle Toms." During the riots, Cleage refused a request to use his influence to tell rioters to cease. But Cleage believed that there were possible areas of cooperation between blacks and New Detroit.[4] With that advice in mind, Hudson decided to include three militants recommended at the meeting among the nine blacks to be appointed to the New Detroit Committee: Lorenzo "Rennie" Freeman, an organizer with the West Central Organization, which drew its inspiration from famed left-wing radical Saul Alinsky and described itself as being prepared to use "unacceptable tactics";

1. Terry, "Action from the Boundary," 168.
2. DIM working with black militants before this from Terry, "Action from the Boundary," 279.
3. Times Staff, "The Rev. Milton Henry," 87.
    Taifa, "Republic of New Afrika."
4. Fine, *Violence in the Model City*, 25, 43, 184, and 321.

Alvin Harrison, a black nationalist who advocated for "break[ing] car and store windows," and was awaiting trial for his role in an earlier race riot in 1966; and 18-year-old Norvell Harrington, who thought no one over 25 should be trusted, described democracy as "trash," and threatened to set ablaze Ford and General Motors if militants weren't given what they want.[5]

It's important to note that these views were not even close to mainstream in the black community. In 1968, only 1 percent of Detroit blacks favored "total separation" of the races while 88 percent supported integration. Only 3.5 percent approved of a separate black nation. Meanwhile, Detroit blacks who lived in the areas of the city affected by the riots gave the highest approval ratings to conventional politicians like Charles Diggs (27 percent) and John Conyers (22 percent), while Albert Cleage was supported by only 4 percent. Though 77 percent of riot-area blacks had heard of Cleage, only 4 percent rated him as "doing the most good" for blacks.[6]

So why include these black nationalists on the New Detroit Committee? Especially while also excluding major mainstream black organizations such as the Booker T. Washington Businessmen's Association and the Council of Baptist Ministers, despite their objections and desire to be included. The New Detroit Committee was accused of participating in "riot insurance." Looking at New Detroit's grantees, that description makes sense. On the first day it was incorporated, New Detroit made a no-strings-attached $50,000 grant to ultra-militant Frank Ditto and his organization

---

5. Fine, *Violence in the Model City*, 136 and 321–322.
    Alvin Harrison quoted in Fine, *Violence in the Model City*, 137.
    West Central Organization details from Fine, *Violence in the Model City*, 30.
    Harrington threatened to set ablaze Ford and GM from Fine, *Violence in the Model City*, 376.
6. Fine, *Violence in the Model City*, 370 and 374.

East Side Voices for Independent Detroit. Ditto had called for "revolution against 'white tyranny' by violent, bloody, or whatever means necessary to 'overthrow the system.'" A New Detroit spokesman described Ditto as "damn controversial," but also "a real guy" who could be "useful" to New Detroit. Ditto commented that "they know if there aren't some crumbs on the table, [the militants] might burn down some shit." Ditto would eventually receive around $250,000 in grants from New Detroit and would be put on its board even as black moderates sought in vain to have him removed. There was "an overwhelming consensus" among New Detroit's trustees— excluding "senior Black Establishment members"—that the militant presence in New Detroit had been "crucial to peacemaking."[7]

Looking back a few years later in 1973, New Detroit's leaders would recognize:

Historically, New Detroit policy on community organization has been the product more of a political, rather than a rational process. Since 1968 a handful of "black community leaders" have been keeping common sense at bay with deft applications of insults and embraces. The ever present need for black community representation and, to some extent, black radical representation in the New Detroit coalition has resulted in a situation in which NDI policy has been pretty much the doings of local proposal writers. That is, anything that could be sold as being new or innovative stood a good chance of being funded, if it was presented forcefully enough or by the right person.[8]

---

7. Fine, *Violence in the Model City*, 322–323 and 380.
8. Colding, "Memo To: Lawrence P. Doss & Walter Douglass."

Hudson, however, denied the riot insurance explanation, claiming that he and his associates understood that no single group had caused or controlled the riot, or could guarantee that there would not be another. Instead, Hudson believed that the "voices" of the militants had to be heard, and hoped that they would "sensitize" the whites on the committee.[9]

This goal of "sensitizing" whites to militant black separatist ideas could be seen in the founding of a subsidiary of New Detroit, Inc., named "New Perspectives on Race, Inc." New Perspectives on Race (NPR) worked to help "educate" whites on racism. It would be New Detroit, Inc., via NPR, that would publish Pat Bidol's curriculum—where "Power + Prejudice" was used for the first time.

But why would Bidol come up with that definition? What exactly were the black separatist ideas she was sensitized with? The answer can be found in Stokely Carmichael and Charles V. Hamilton's 1967 book *Black Power: The Politics of Liberation in America.*

---

9. Fine, *Violence in the Model City*, 321 and 322.

Who Was Stokely Carmichael?

Stokely Carmichael was a self-described Marxist-Leninist. He developed his "political consciousness" in the 1950s through his friendship with the son of the leader of the local Communist Party. His favorite philosophers in college were Marx and Engels.[1] Carmichael was welcomed to Cuba by Fidel Castro in 1967 (only a few years after the Cuban Missile Crisis) and would continue to praise Castro as late as 1998, shortly before Carmichael's death.[2] In 1968 he moved to Guinea to dedicate the remainder of his life to forming a communist pan-African black ethnostate and renamed himself "Kwame Ture," to honor Ghanaian president Kwame Nkrumah, a Marxist-Leninist who proclaimed solidarity with the Soviet Union and the Mao-era People's Republic of China, and Guinean president Ahmed Sékou Touré, a Marxist who ruled for 28 years until his death and killed an estimated 50,000 political

---

1. Lamb, "Life and Career of Kwame Ture."
2. Gray, "Hell Yes We Are Going to Lybia!"
   Garrow, "The Tragedy of Stokely Carmichael," 566.

opponents in concentration camps.[3] Carmichael also cultivated close personal friendships with Ugandan president, Soviet ally, and mass murderer Idi Amin (estimates of the deaths under Amin's regime range between 100,000 and 500,000) and Libyan socialist dictator and terrorism sponsor Muammar Gaddafi.[4]

Carmichael gained fame in America as the leader of the Student Nonviolent Coordinating Committee (SNCC). The group had previously been led by civil rights icon and future congressman John Lewis, but Lewis left after Carmichael gained leadership and dismissed the group's nonviolence.[5] Carmichael explained:

> we used the name 'nonviolent' because at that time Martin Luther King was the central figure of the black struggle and he was still preaching nonviolence, and anyone who talked about violence at that time was considered treasonable—amounting—to treason, so we decided that we would use the name nonviolent, but in the meantime we knew our struggle was not about to be nonviolent.[6]

Carmichael started his career in the civil rights movement as a much less radical figure than the militant separatist he would become. Yet despite King having said kind words about Carmichael and King's Southern Christian Leadership Conference awarding Carmichael a college scholarship, Carmichael's radicalism grew to

---

3. South African History Online, "Dr Kwame Nkrumah."
    BBC News "'Mass Graves' Found in Guinea."
4. Garrow, "The Tragedy of Stokely Carmichael," 569.
    Ullman, "Human Rights and Economic Power."
5. Digital Gateway, "Stokely Carmichael Elected as SNCC's Chair."
6. Congress, Senate, Committee on the Judiciary, *Testimony of Stokely Carmichael.*

such a point that it led him to accuse King of "Uncle Tomism."[7]
King, in his final book *Where Do We Go From Here: Chaos or
Community,* openly criticized Carmichael by name and his views on
"Black Power" in the book's longest chapter.[8]

President Johnson was particularly concerned about
Carmichael, at one point ordering the FBI to send him reports on
Carmichael several times a week.[9] During the long, hot summer of
1967, Johnson was originally inclined to believe there was an
"organized conspiracy" behind the riots. Though the Kerner
Commission found no incitement, when investigating they "ran
Stokely Carmichael's comings and goings through a computer."[10]
The Kerner Report did include a story of Carmichael's influence on
a riot, and it reinforces his and SNCC's ideological distance from
the vast majority of the African American community:

> The headquarters of the Student Nonviolent
> Coordinating Committee (SNCC) is located in
> Atlanta. Its former president, Stokely Carmichael,
> wearing a green Malcolm X sweatshirt, appeared,
> together with several companions. Approaching a
> police captain, Carmichael asked why there were so
> many police cars in the area. Informed that they were
> there to make sure there was no disturbance,
> Carmichael, clapping his hands, declared in a sing-
> song voice that there might have to be a riot if the

---

7. Martin Luther King Jr. Research and Education Institute, "Carmichael, Stokely."
    Carmichael accused King of "Uncle Tomism" from Pilgrim, "The Tom
Caricature."
8. King, *Where Do We Go from Here?,* chap. 2.
9. Chen, "LBJ Targeted Black Power Radicals."
10. U.S. National Advisory Commission on Civil Disorders, *The Kerner Report,*
intro.

police cars were not removed. When Carmichael refused to move on as requested, he was arrested.

Soon released on bail, the next morning Carmichael declared that the black people were preparing to resist "armed aggression" by the police by whatever means necessary.

Shortly thereafter in the Dixie Hills Shopping Center, which had been closed down for the day, a Negro youth, using a broom handle, began to pound on the outside bell of a burglar alarm that had been set off, apparently, by a short circuit. Police officers responded to the alarm and ordered him to stop hitting the bell. A scuffle ensued. Several bystanders intervened. One of the officers drew his service revolver and fired, superficially wounding the young man.

Tensions rose. Approximately 250 persons were present at that evening's meeting. When a number of Negro leaders urged the submission of a petition of grievances through legal channels, the response was lukewarm. When Carmichael took the podium, urging Negroes "to take to the streets and force the police department to work until they fall in their tracks," the response was tumultuous.

The press quoted him as saying: "It's not a question of law and order. We are not concerned with peace. We are concerned with the liberation of black people. We have to build a revolution."

As the people present at the meeting poured into the street, they were joined by others. The crowd soon numbered an estimated 1,000. From alleys and rooftops rocks and bottles were thrown at the nine police officers on the scene. Windows of police cars were broken. Firecrackers exploded in the darkness. Police believe they may have been fired on.

Reinforced by approximately 60 to 70 officers, the police, firing over the heads of the crowd, quickly regained control. Of the 10 persons arrested, six were 21 years of age or younger; only one was in his thirties.

The next day city equipment arrived in the area to begin work on the long-delayed playgrounds and other projects demanded by the citizens. It was announced that a Negro Youth patrol would be established along the lines of the Tampa White Hats.

SNCC responded that volunteers for the patrol would be selling their "black brothers out," and would be viewed as "black traitors," to be dealt with in the "manner we see fit." Nevertheless, during the course of the summer, the 200 youths participating in the corps played an important role in preventing a serious outbreak. The police believe that establishment of the youth corps became a major factor in improving police-community relations.[11]

The end result for Carmichael was that "within the next few days a petition was drawn up by State Senator Leroy Johnson and other moderate Negro leaders demanding that Stokely Carmichael get out of the community and allow the people to handle their own affairs. It was signed by more than 1,000 persons in the Dixie Hills area."[12]

---

11. U.S. National Advisory Commission on Civil Disorders, *The Kerner Report*, 69.
12. U.S. National Advisory Commission on Civil Disorders, *The Kerner Report*, 70.
Despite common repetition in recent times of Martin Luther King Jr.'s quote "riots are the language of the unheard," King and other African American leaders

Carmichael was also friends with Louis Farrakhan and worked with, and would be honored by, the Nation of Islam, a group that the left-wing Southern Poverty Law Center has identified as a hate group.[13] In 1968, Carmichael joined the Black Panther Party, a violent organization associated with multiple murders, as their "Honorary Prime Minister."[14] However, Carmichael was too radical for even the Black Panthers, splitting with them over whether white activists should be allowed to participate in the movement; the Panthers believed they should, but Carmichael believed they should not.

Eighteen months after Malcolm X's murder, a 1966 New York Times profile of Carmichael noted that "some have begun to describe him as a new Malcolm X."[15] But before his death, Malcolm X had changed his views substantially on working with whites:

> Brother, remember the time that white college girl came into the restaurant—the one who wanted to help the [black] Muslims and the whites get together—and I told her there wasn't a ghost of a chance and she went away crying? Well, I've lived to regret that

---

were in fact forcefully opposed to rioting. King wrote in 1967, "it is understandable that the white community should fear the outbreak of riots. They are indefensible as weapons of struggle, and Negroes must sympathize with whites who feel menaced by them. Indeed, Negroes are themselves no less menaced, and those living in the ghetto always suffer most directly from the destructive turbulence of a riot." King, *Where Do We Go from Here?*, 22.

For examples of recent claims that King supported rioting, see Woodson, *What Martin Luther King REALLY Thought About Riots.*

13. Umoja, *Tribute to Kwame Turé.*
   Southern Poverty Law Center, "Nation of Islam."
14. Anthony, "Black Power's Coolest Radicals (but Also a Gang of Ruthless Killers)."
   Kaufman, "Stokely Carmichael, Rights Leader Who Coined 'Black Power,' Dies at 57."
15. Garrow, "The Tragedy of Stokely Carmichael." 564.

incident. In many parts of the African continent I saw white students helping black people. Something like this kills a lot of argument. I did many things as a [black] Muslim that I'm sorry for now. I was a zombie then—like all [black] Muslims—I was hypnotized, pointed in a certain direction and told to march. Well, I guess a man's entitled to make a fool of himself if he's ready to pay the cost. It cost me 12 years.

That was a bad scene, brother. The sickness and madness of those days—I'm glad to be free of them.[16]

Sadly, Carmichael never seemed to learn that lesson and would work toward his separatist mission until his death in 1998.

In his book *Black Power*, on the first page of the first chapter, Carmichael defined racism in a way that laid the groundwork for the "Power + Prejudice" definition, though without using those words:

What is racism? The word has represented daily reality to millions of black people for centuries, yet it is rarely defined—perhaps just because that reality has been such a commonplace. By "racism" we mean the predication of decisions and policies on considerations of race for the purpose of *subordinating* a racial group and maintaining control over that group. That has been the practice of this country toward the black man; we shall see why and how.

Contrary to Carmichael's claims, racism was commonly defined and in a different way than his definition. *Webster's Seventh New Collegiate Dictionary*, published in 1963, defined "racism" as "(1) a

16. Parks, "'I Was A Zombie Back Then—Like All Muslims I Was Hypnotized.'"

belief that race is the primary determinant of human traits and capacities and that racial differences produce an inherent superiority of a particular race. (2) RACIALISM." "Racialism", explicitly a synonym for racism, was defined as "(1) racial prejudice or discrimination. (2) RACISM."[17]

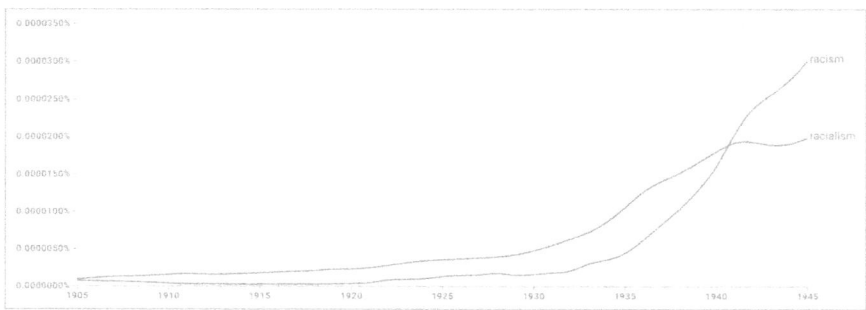

Percentage of all ngrams (series of adjacent characters) in millions of scanned books that were "racism" or "racialism," 1905-1945.

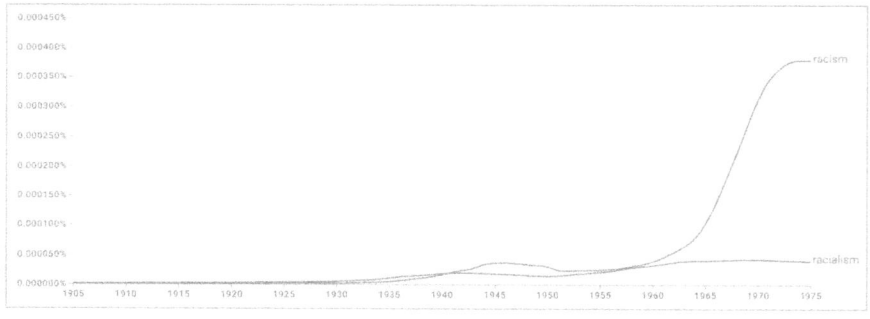

Percentage of all ngrams (series of adjacent characters) in millions of scanned books that were "racism" or "racialism," 1905–1975.

The *New Miriam-Webster Pocket Dictionary*, a more consumer-

---

17. *Webster's Seventh New Collegiate Dictionary,* "racism."
    Google, "Google Books Ngram Viewer, 'racism, racialism.'"

oriented dictionary published in 1964, struck "racialism" entirely and defined racism as "a belief that some races are by nature superior to others; also: discrimination based on such belief".[18]

Webster's New World Dictionary of the American Language, published in 1966 and specifically designed for our nation's use of language, defined racism as "1. racialism. 2. program or practice of racial discrimination, segregation, persecution and domination, based on racialism." "Racialism" was defined as "a doctrine or feeling of racial differences or antagonisms, especially with reference to supposed racial superiority, inferiority, or purity; racial prejudice, hatred, or discrimination."[19]

Even in British English, the definition was similar; Sheffield City Libraries' *'ISMS: A Dictionary of Words Ending in -ISM, -OLOGY and -PHOBIA,* published in 1963, didn't include "racism" but did include "racialism," which it defined as "a programme or practice of racial discrimination, segregation, persecution, and domination."[20]

As far back as 1933, *The Oxford English Dictionary* defined "racialism" as "tendency to racial feeling; antagonism between different races of men" and a "racialist" as "one who fosters racialism."[21] In 1989 it revised the definition of "racialism" to "Belief in the superiority of a particular race leading to prejudice and antagonism towards people of other races, esp. those in close proximity who may be felt as a threat to one's cultural and racial integrity or economic well-being" and did not alter that definition

18. *The New Merriam-Webster Pocket Dictionary,* "racism."
19. *Webster's New World Dictionary of the American Language,* "racism."
20. *'ISMS,* "racialism."
21. Murray et al., *The Oxford English Dictionary Being a Corrected Re-Issue,* "racialism."

until 2008, at which point it was changed to "= RACISM n. An earlier term than RACISM n., but now largely superseded by it."[22]

Not one of those definitions include as a requirement that racism be about "maintaining control" over a group, nor that the "subordination" (or domination) inherent in racism must be directed toward the entire racial group rather than simply individuals within it. Racial prejudice or discrimination stated in some form or another was, and still is, the most common dictionary definition. Today, proponents of the "Power + Prejudice" definition often argue that dictionary definitions don't matter if there is a different definition used by experts in academia.[23] But at this time in history, the definition in question had not yet been created. So regardless of the merit or lack thereof of that argument, it cannot hold in this case. Dictionary definitions are not arbitrary or fabricated—they seek to record the existing usage of words. Carmichael was clearly redefining the word away from its commonly understood meaning. Why?

Without a stated reason, it's impossible to know Carmichael's thinking. But it may have something to do with being the founder of the notion of "institutional racism," and describing it for the first time immediately after his definition of racism above:

 Racism is both overt and covert. It takes two, closely related forms: individual whites acting against individual blacks, and acts by the total white community against the black community. We call these individual racism and institutional racism. The first consists of overt acts by individuals which cause

---

22. Oxford English Dictionary, "Discover the Story of English."
23. See this example from an activist author: OnlyBlackGirl, "Your Dictionary Definition of Racism Is Outdated Trash."

death, injury or the violent destruction of property. This type can be recorded by television cameras; it can frequently be observed in the process of commission. The second type is less overt, far more subtle, less identifiable in terms of *specific* individuals committing the acts. But it is no less destructive of human life. The second type originates in the operation of established and respected forces in the society, and this receives far less public condemnation than the first type. ...

Institutional racism relies on the active and pervasive operation of anti-black attitudes and practices. A sense of superior group position prevails: whites are "better" than blacks; therefore blacks should be subordinated to whites. This is a racist attitude and it permeates the society, on both the individual and institutional level, covertly and overtly.

"Respectable" individuals can absolve themselves from individual blame: *they* would never plant a bomb in a church; *they* would never stone a black family. But they continue to support political officials and institutions that would and do perpetuate institutionally racist policies. Thus *acts* of overt individual racism may not typify the society, but institutional racism does—with the support of covert, individual *attitudes* of racism.[24]

Although already implicitly defining racism as something that only whites can do against blacks, rather than in any direction, the concept of institutional racism as described by Carmichael is,

24. Carmichael and Hamilton, *Black Power*, 20–21.

overall, mostly accurate and useful. There are clear cases of institutional racism in American history. Thinking beyond individual slave owners, slavery involved racist laws, racist institutions enforcing those laws, and the support of a larger populace to keep those laws and institutions in place; the same with Jim Crow. And as the Kerner Commission found, racist institutions were implicated in the creation of the ghetto. This valuable concept can help us better understand how racism can work, which helps explain why it caught on in academia.

But in the hands of a communist who has repeated the mantra of "from each according to his ability to each according to his need," institutional racism is a severely dangerous concept.[25] To someone who believes that merit should play no role in one's success and that full equality of outcome should be the norm regardless of inputs, "covert, individual attitudes of racism" need only mean society sanctioning institutions where racial representation isn't perfectly equal. Schools, universities, or businesses having unequal representation of blacks can be labeled as institutionally racist simply on the grounds of having a disparity—without any need to inquire *why*. Is the disparity in representation caused by racist obstacles, or is there another reason? For example, cultural differences between communities leading to less-qualified or less-interested candidates, or a reduced number of fathers present in the black community leading to worse long-term life outcomes. Thousands of potential factors could lead to different outcomes without overt racism playing a role, but the communist focus on "equality of outcome" removes any need to track down traditional overt racism somewhere in the chain leading up to institutional racism. This allows Carmichael and those following him to use institutional racism as a blunt instrument, to level accusations of

---

25. Lamb, "Life and Career of Kwame Ture," 25:06.

racism even where it might not exist, and as proof that all of white society is complicit in institutional racism—unless they ally themselves to the destructive effort to replace American society with Carmichael's vision of a racialized communist utopia. And that is indeed how Carmichael used it, approvingly quoting Charles Silberman's *Crisis in Black and White*:

> What we are discovering, in short, is that the United States—all of it, North as well as South, West as well as East—is a racist society in a sense and to a degree that we have refused so far to admit, much less face. ... The tragedy of race relations in the United States is that there is no American Dilemma. White Americans are not torn and tortured by the conflict between their devotion to the American creed and their actual behavior.[26]

That Carmichael's definition requires a desire to "subordinate" and "maintain control" creates exceptions to what qualifies as institutional racism that are convenient for his argument. Attempting to form a black ethno-state, which would necessarily deny all other races equal citizenship or immigration opportunities, cannot be institutionally racist if its purpose is only to lift up blacks rather than subordinate whites. Any opposition to integration along those lines is free from "racism" under Carmichael's definition.

---

26. Carmichael and Hamilton, *Black Power*, 21.

Note the ellipses in there. From page 10 of *Crisis in Black and White*, this is the text that Carmichael excluded: "Twenty years ago, Gunnar Myrdal concluded that 'the American Negro problem is a problem in the heart of the American,' and titled his monumental study of the Negro *An American Dilemma*. Myrdal was wrong." Although Carmichael and Silberman were on the same page, it is interesting that Carmichael chose to exclude content that named an example of a credible view that was contrary to his and Silberman's own. Silberman, *Crisis in Black and White*, 10.

Carmichael used his book to argue, against the desires of the vast majority of African Americans, that "the goal of black people must *not* be to assimilate into middle-class America, for that class—as a whole—is without a viable conscience as regards humanity."[27]

Carmichael was a radical anti-integrationist. He believed integration "is a subterfuge for the maintenance of white supremacy" and:

> "Integration" also means that black people must give up their identity, deny their heritage. ... "At the present time, integration as a solution to the race problem demands the Negro foreswear his identity as a Negro." The fact is that integration, as traditionally articulated, would abolish the black community. ... The racial and cultural personality of the black community must be preserved and that community must win its freedom while preserving its cultural integrity.[28]

The language Carmichael uses bears a shocking resemblance to that of white nationalists, such as Sam Francis, who said, "instead of invoking a suicidal liberalism and regurgitating the very universalism that has subverted our identity and our sense of solidarity, what we as whites must do is reassert our identity and our solidarity."[29] Carmichael wrote of blacks who wanted to integrate into middle-class society: "Such people will state that they would prefer to be treated 'only as individuals, not as Negroes'; that they 'are not and should not be preoccupied with race.' This is a totally unrealistic

27. Carmichael and Hamilton, *Black Power*, 40.
28. Carmichael and Hamilton, *Black Power*, 47.
29. AR Staff, "Sam Francis in His Own Words."
    Southern Poverty Law Center, "Sam Francis."

position. In the first place, black people have not suffered as individuals but as members of a group; therefore their liberation lies in group action."[30] Meanwhile, white nationalist Jared Taylor similarly wrote, "the racial consciousness that is vital for European survival is not strong enough to break through smothering layers of sham democracy because identitarian instincts have been destroyed by bourgeois individualism."[31]

It appears Carmichael's idiosyncratic redefinition of the term racism was created to forward his preexisting radical separatist agenda, not as a politically neutral academic tool to better study racism. Even if it were, Carmichael's extremist views should have been enough to prevent scholars from taking his redefinition too seriously. Ultimately, Carmichael was indifferent to whether or not the society that resulted from his fight against white "institutional racism" ended up racist itself, writing, "in the end, we cannot and shall not offer any guarantees that Black Power, if achieved, would be non-racist. No one can predict human behavior. Social change always has unanticipated consequences. If black racism is what the larger society fears, we cannot help them."[32]

But Carmichael's influence on white anti-racists went beyond his redefinition, also including active instructions for prospective white activists. Prior to writing *Black Power*, a vote by SNCC leadership expelled whites from the group.[33] Although the vote was not a priority for Carmichael (it was pushed by SNCC's "Atlanta Project") he agreed that the condition of whiteness made allyship difficult, "no matter how 'liberal' a white person might be, he cannot escape the overpowering influence—on himself and on black people —of his whiteness in a racist society. Liberal whites often say that

---

30. Carmichael and Hamilton, *Black Power*, 47.
31. Taylor, "Why We Fight."
32. Carmichael and Hamilton, *Black Power*, 45.
33. Digital Gateway, "SNCC Staff Meeting at Peg Leg Bates Club."

they are tired of being told 'you can't understand what it is to be black.' They claim to recognize and acknowledge this. Yet those same liberals will often turn around and tell black people that they should ally themselves with those who can't understand, who share a sense of superiority based on whiteness."[34] Instead, Carmichael had different ideas for how whites could help in the Black Power movement:

 At the beginning of our discussion of Black Power, we said that black people must redefine themselves, state new values and goals. The same holds true for white people of good will; they too need to redefine themselves and their role.

Some people see the advocates of Black Power as concerned with ridding the civil rights struggle of white people. This has been untrue from the beginning. There is a definite, much-needed role whites can play. This role can best be examined on three different, yet interrelated, levels: educative, organizational, supportive. **Given the pervasive nature of racism in the society and the extent to which attitudes of white superiority and black inferiority have become embedded, it is very necessary that white people begin to disabuse themselves of such notions**. Black people, as we stated earlier, will lead the challenge to old values and norms, but whites who recognize the need must also work in this sphere. Whites have access to groups in the society never reached by black people. They must

34. Carmichael and Hamilton, *Black Power*, 52.

get within those groups and help perform this essential educative function.

One of the most disturbing things about almost all white supporters has been that they are reluctant to go into their own communities—which is where the racism exists—and work to get rid of it. We are not now speaking of whites who have worked to get black people "accepted," on an individual basis, by the white society. Of these there have been many; their efforts are undoubtedly well-intended and individually helpful. But too often those efforts are geared to the same false premises as integration; too often the society in which they seek acceptance of a few black people can afford to make the gesture. We are speaking, rather, of those whites who see the need for basic change and have hooked up with the black liberation movement because it seemed the most promising agent of such change. Yet they often admonish black people to be non-violent. They should preach non-violence in the white community. Where possible, they might also educate other white people to the need for Black Power. The range is great, with much depending on the white person's own class background and environment.

On a broader scale, there is the very important function of working to reorient this society's attitudes and policies towards African and Asian countries. **Across the country, smug white communities show a poverty of awareness, a poverty of humanity, indeed, a poverty of ability to act in a civilized manner towards non-Anglo human beings. The white**

middle-class   suburbs   need   "freedom schools"   as   badly   as   the   black communities. Anglo-conformity is a dead weight on their necks too. All this is an educative role crying to be performed by those whites so inclined.[35]

In post-riot Detroit, a number of whites were willing to take on that "educative role" of teaching Carmichael's idiosyncratic separatist views to other whites. Pat Bidol was one of them, but she was predated by other attempts.

---

35. Carmichael and Hamilton, *Black Power*, 62.
    Emphasis added.

Detroit's "Anti-Racist" Activists

New Detroit-aligned militant Albert Cleage was a big supporter of Carmichael, telling his church "to stop being 'House Niggers and slaves like Whitney Young [executive director of the National Urban League] and Roy Wilkins [executive director of the NAACP] and to stand and fight like Stokley [sic] Carmichael,'" demonstrating how Carmichael's influence could spread within New Detroit.[1]

People Against Racism was founded in Detroit by Frank Joyce prior to the 1967 riots. Joyce was an active supporter of Carmichael's SNCC, but after SNCC expelled its white members, Joyce dedicated his efforts to spreading Carmichael-style views on racism within the white community. Joyce cited Carmichael regularly in his writings. Referring to white people, Joyce said "we have met the enemy—and he is us."[2] Like Carmichael, Joyce

1. Fine, *Violence in the Model City*, 143.
    Encyclopaedia Britannica, "Roy Wilkins."
    Encyclopaedia Britannica, "Whitney M. Young, Jr."
2. Hurwitz and Snook, "Pilot Study," 61.

believed that "integration has failed ... partly because the terms under which it has been posed are themselves white supremacist" and that "all American white institutions are racist, or more accurately, white supremacist, and all operate to perpetuate white privilege."[3]

Joyce also worked to redefine racism along his own lines, refining Carmichael's communist-based conception of institutional racism into the more bluntly defined "behavioral racism," which Joyce explained "may be defined as any action, individual or institutional, which disadvantaged non-whites to the advantage of whites, *regardless of conscious motivation*."[4] Joyce explained in more recent writings that "to this day, many liberals and radicals think that well-meaning whites should support policies that 'help' African Americans. Among other problems, this carries within it the deeply embedded notion that there is something 'wrong' with blacks and nothing 'wrong' with whites. To put it another way, the problem isn't the *effects* of racism, although they surely exist. The problem is the racism itself."

At its peak, People Against Racism had full-time staff in several cities and chapters on 25 campuses.[5] Although People Against Racism has since dissolved, Joyce remains alive and active in far-left politics, having called famed African American neurosurgeon and

---

3. Joyce, "An Analysis of American Racism," 2 and 4.
4. Joyce, "An Analysis of American Racism," 3.
    While this essay focuses on the popular "Power + Prejudice" redefinition of racism, another popular redefinition sharing much of the same ideological lineage, that advocated by bestselling author Ibram X. Kendi, sounds like Joyce's. Kendi defines a racist as "one who is supporting a racist policy through their actions or inaction or expressing a racist idea" and a "racist policy" as "any measure that produces or sustains racial inequity between racial groups." Kendi, Ibram X. "Ibram X. Kendi Defines What It Means to Be an Antiracist."
5. Joyce, "It's Time to Change the Water in the Fish Tank."

Secretary of Housing and Urban Development Ben Carson a "white supremacist" during his 2016 run for president.[6]

The most influential person on the development of Racism Awareness Training was Robert William Terry, a white man and Detroit Industrial Mission employee. While it's rare to see his work referenced today, Terry's philosophy on race and racism is strikingly similar to the ideas that would take off decades later within academic "Critical Whiteness Studies." They are so similar, in fact, that it seems impossible that the founders of Critical Whiteness Studies weren't aware of his work, or at least influenced by those who were. Upon discovering Terry's work, Critical Whiteness Studies professor Say Burgin worried that the striking similarity might be "an indication that white racial justice activism had not evolved much in the past four decades," noting that she was "puzzled as to why I had never heard of Terry" and troubled by his absence in the body of work of Critical Whiteness Studies.[7]

Terry joined DIM in 1967, but the organization was founded over a decade earlier, in 1956.[8] It was started by Episcopalian Reverend Hugh White and began with the goal of recruiting groups of industrial workers "to discuss the relationships between the Christian faith and problems of daily work in Industry." This goal would change over time, eventually leading to DIM describing its purpose as being a "social justice change agent" during Terry's tenure.[9] White believed that "the industrial world in which we exist is confused in its understanding of such major axioms as justice, freedom, authority, status, money, race, power, etc."[10] The Mission considered itself a descendant of the Social Gospel Movement, a

6.   Joyce, "White Men Must Be Stopped."
7.   Burgin, Locating Douglass Fitch," 3–4.
8.   Terry, "Action from the Boundary," 20 and 276.
9.   Terry, "Action from the Boundary," 44 and 420.
10. Terry, "Action from the Boundary," 52.

Protestant movement of the late 1800s and early 1900s that focused on issues of social justice such as economic inequality, the environment, and war.[11] The Social Gospel Movement was heavily socialist in nature, with movement leader Walter Rauschenbusch promoting "Christian socialism" and believing "God had to raise up socialism because the organized Church was too blind, or too slow, to realize God's ends."[12] Similarly, DIM believed that "men could not be healed apart from the social structures in which they worked and lived" and thus defined itself as "a Mission to the structures which shape man and set the context for man's destruction or his fulfillment" as opposed to engaging in personal counseling or pastoral care.[13]

At first, DIM had difficulty gaining access to industry to accomplish those ends. Industry treated DIM with suspicion due to the social gospel tradition of labor organizing and attacking management. However, DIM's goal was not to organize labor, and with effort, they were able to overcome industry's skepticism.[14] The Mission stayed out of any policy decisions relating to management or the unions, and for many years they stayed out of controversial social issues as well.[15] For example, despite all members of the Mission being supporters of civil rights, for many years they were afraid to take any action on it for fear of becoming involved in a public controversy and losing their access to industry.[16] This cautious tactic would prove effective. By the mid-60s, DIM had gained sufficient access within industry to hold overnight retreats

---

11. Terry, "Action from the Boundary," 32.
    Social Gospel definition from Tichi, *Civic Passions*.
12. Feuerherd, "When Christian Evangelicals Loved Socialism."
13. Terry, "Action from the Boundary," 29.
14. Terry, "Action from the Boundary," 65–66.
15. Terry, "Action from the Boundary," 73.
16. Terry, "Action from the Boundary," 118.

with staff from Ford, Chrysler, Dodge, and others.[17] DIM would be considered successful enough that they would inspire the creation of further industrial missions in cities around the nation.[18]

DIM's staff did not unanimously agree on the cautious approach. Mission staff member Scott Paradise consistently attempted to push his coworkers in a more radical direction, believing that "Christian integrity and by implication DIM's integrity would be sacrificed if it conformed to the prevailing cultural ethos." His socialist leanings made it difficult for him to accept the capitalist presuppositions of the industrial organizations DIM desired to work with.[19] The rest of the staff found him politically naïve, but they admired him for his ability to work with labor rank and file, radical labor activists, and members of the general community.[20] When Paradise gave testimony before the State Affairs Committee on Civil Rights Legislation that was perceived as "too radical," DIM was temporarily expelled from Ford, which angered DIM's board members.[21] However, despite the Ford incident, overall, DIM still continued to build its institutional legitimacy; in 1964, Hugh White was invited by Governor Romney to sit on "a special Governor's Committee to study the workmen's compensation law of the state and recommend legislative action."[22]

But as time passed, DIM staff became progressively more involved in social issues. In September 1966, three members of the staff, Robert Batchelder, Jesse Christman, and James Campbell, were arrested while participating in "demonstrations" sponsored by the West Central Organization. Batchelder recalled:

---

17. Terry, "Action from the Boundary," 139.
18. Terry, "Action from the Boundary," 148.
19. Terry, "Action from the Boundary," 202.
20. Terry, "Action from the Boundary," 159.
21. Terry, "Action from the Boundary," 222 and 230.
22. Terry, "Action from the Boundary," 233.

> The events of September 1966 involved a series of demonstrations focused upon a city-owned house on an urban renewal site. On three separate occasions, demonstrators were arrested by the police on charges of trespassing and assault and battery. This action included the participation of 150 clergy who marched upon the mayor's office seeking changes in the city policy having to do with the relocation of persons in urban renewal sites and changes in the treatment of persons arrested in such demonstrations. When a consultation with the mayor failed to yield any progress the 150 clergymen moved as a body to a city-owned house on Hobart Street, tore off the boards which the Detroit Housing Commission had used to close up the house, and proceeded to make the house clean, repaired, and inhabitable for a large family needing adequate housing. These events had a prominent place in the headlines of the Detroit papers over a period of weeks.[23]

Although DIM staff participated in the event as individuals, not as official Mission work, the event became a meaningful symbol among staff. Those arrested relished opportunities to share what the event meant to them with new staff members.[24]

By late 1966, DIM felt that it had gained sufficient access within industry that it should adopt "more flexible and change-oriented methods," desiring to be "change agents." Thus, the discussion groups that had formed the core of their operations "were replaced by planned change curricula, consulting skills, and action/research

---

23. Terry, "Action from the Boundary," 279.
24. Terry, "Action from the Boundary," 280.

all designed to service industrial clients on a mutually negotiated basis."[25] Previously, the Mission had taught industry staff by discussing moral dilemmas like "what happens, for instance, when quality of production must be sacrificed for quantity?" Or, "how does a manager resolve conflict between home obligations and work obligations?" But DIM became unsatisfied with the impact of these sorts of lessons, wanting to change industrial structures more than anything else. To accomplish this, its new curriculums attempted to bring in the insights of "sensitivity training."[26]

25. Terry, "Action from the Boundary," 238.
26. Terry, "Action from the Boundary," 246.

The National Training Laboratories and "Sensitivity Training"

The Detroit Industrial Mission's work with the National Training Laboratories (NTL) goes back to at least 1963, when Scott Paradise traveled to its headquarters in Bethel, Maine, to participate in NTL's "sensitivity training laboratory." In the years that followed, more DIM staff followed in his footsteps to Bethel.[1] Despite Paradise's views being at odds with much of the DIM staff, after he returned from his sensitivity training, "he experienced that he could work in a group without alienating all the [other staff] members."[2]

What is "sensitivity training," and what is the National Training Laboratories? To properly answer those questions, we must first look to "the Father of NTL," psychologist Kurt Lewin.[3]

Lewin, who headed the "psychological warfare center for the Far East" at the Office of Strategic Services (a predecessor to the

---

1. Terry, "Action from the Boundary," 161 and 166.
2. Terry, "Action from the Boundary," 161. Terry cites back to "Paradise, Journal, XVII (March 17, 1963–September 30, 1963), 37."
3. Bradford, *National Training Laboratories*, 4.

Central Intelligence Agency) during WWII, is perhaps best known for his research on "group dynamics"—the psychology of how people act within social groups and the interactions between social groups.[4] Lewin developed the principle of "force field analysis," a framework used to study the factors that influence social groups to move toward their goals and those that block groups from achieving their goals.[5]

Lewin also focused his career on studying how people change and come to accept new values via "re-education." He believed that new belief systems and values are often accepted when people feel a sense of belonging after joining a new social group, upon which "previously rejected facts will become accepted as they become 'facts' of 'his group.'" This re-education influences a person's conduct so long as their new beliefs and values dominate their perceptions.[6] Although Lewin worked decades before the advent of postmodernism, his worldview was quite similar to that of many postmodernist philosophers, espousing a "social constructivist view that reality is shaped by what is socially accepted as reality."[7] His re-educative change process involved "unfreezing" people's previously held psychological patterns, moving them to "a new level" of thoughts, feelings, and/or behavior, and then "refreezing" that change.[8] Lewin's view was that "the primary task of reeducation involves a change in the person's social perception." To create "changes in knowledge, values, and beliefs," a person must first change their perception of themselves and the situations they're in.[9] To accomplish this, a simple acceptance of new facts isn't enough;

---

4. *Encyclopædia Britannica*, "Kurt Lewin"
   Psychological warfare claim from Bradford, *National Training Laboratories*, 12.
5. Mind Tools, "Force Field Analysis."
6. Daniels, "Kurt Lewin Notes."
7. Coghlan and Jacobs, "Kurt Lewin on Reeducation," 446.
8. Coghlan and Jacobs, "Kurt Lewin on Reeducation," 446.
9. Coghlan and Jacobs, "Kurt Lewin on Reeducation," 448.

people must have total, active involvement in their new values. If only the facts were accepted without full involvement, it could lead to emotional tension and bad conscience. They needed, in his words, a new "action-ideology."[10]

Lewin believed that this sort of re-education could lead to "cultural reconstruction." A moralist as well as a scientist, Lewin held that "it was not enough to try to explain things; one also had to try to change them."[11] "As it applied to democracy (which Lewin strongly supported), for example, Lewin thought democracy "can't be limited to political processes but must be interwoven with every aspect of the culture." Lewin was a founder and the sixth president of the Society for the Psychological Study of Social Issues (Division 9 of the American Psychological Association), a group of "scholar-activists" who used "social science to create a more socially just world." While much of that activism was positive, the first and third presidents of the society were investigated by the House Un-American Activities Committee for their alleged involvement with Communist front organizations.[12] Lewin was committed to bridging the divide that he perceived between "actionists," educators, and scientists.[13]

While he disagreed ideologically with the antidemocratic policies of Soviet Communism, Lewin had substantial Marxist ties, specifically to the Frankfurt School. Though he is not usually considered a member of the Frankfurt School, the neo-Marxist school where Critical Theory was developed, he did work with the Frankfurt School before leaving Germany for America in 1933.[14]

---

10. Coghlan and Jacobs, "Kurt Lewin on Reeducation," 449.
11. Coghlan and Jacobs, "Kurt Lewin on Reeducation," 444.
    Bradford, *National Training Laboratories*, Appendix 4.
12. Society for the Psychological Study of Social Issues, SPSSI Timeline.
13. Bradford, *National Training Laboratories*, Appendix 5.
14. Encyclopedia of Marxism, "Kurt Lewin."

And, as Herbert Marcuse of the Frankfurt School wrote in his famed essay "Repressive Tolerance," Lewin believed that democratic cultures could not be fully tolerant, as they must have "intolerance toward intolerance."[15] Early in his career, Lewin was a friend and collaborator with communist philosopher Karl Korsch, and just before his death in 1947 Lewin proclaimed "Marx was right," referring to Marx's theories of human behavior. [16]

Lewin did not live to see the first operations of NTL in the summer of 1947, but his ideas formed its underlying philosophy, and he gave "enthusiastic support" to its creation, including securing the grant from the Office of Naval Research that supported NTL's first year. He ran the "Connecticut Workshop in Intergroup Relations," the immediate predecessor to NTL.[17]

In 1946, Lewin was asked by the Connecticut Interracial Commission to run a workshop that would help implement a new state law that made certain discriminatory acts illegal and "advance the elimination of discriminatory practices along racial, ethnic, and religious lines."[18] The commission had approached Lewin, a Jew who escaped Germany prior to the Holocaust, because it was dissatisfied with its existing programs and wanted Lewin, who was interested in "interracial issues," to try something new.[19]

Lewin accepted the project in part because he and his team "were dissatisfied with the progress being made in developing a science of individual and group relations," and wanted a real-world situation in order to study "group conflict, group action procedures, the changing of deeply intrenched [sic] attitudes, and the exploring

---

15. Wolff, Barrington, Jr., Marcuse, *A Critique of Pure Tolerance.*
    Encyclopedia of Marxism, "Kurt Lewin."
16. Gerard, "'Marx Was Right.'"
17. Bradford, *National Training Laboratories*, 4.
18. Bradford, *National Training Laboratories*, 19.
19. Bradford, *National Training Laboratories*, 33 and Appendix 5

of bases of apathy in group membership."[20] To help run the program, he brought in three others who had worked with him in various capacities: Ronald Lippitt, Lewin's successor as the head of the psychological warfare center for the Far East at OSS; Leland Bradford, director of the Division of Adult Education Service at the National Education Association (NEA) and the former training director of the Federal Security Agency; and Kenneth (Ken) Benne.[21]

Ken Benne was certainly the most radical member of the group. A democratic socialist, he explained his background as follows:

 I had brought with me from Kansas a somewhat radical orientation to social affairs. ... [My father] had been a Populist in Kansas at the turn of the century, and he believed that we must move beyond competitive capitalism toward some cooperative form of society if the proper conditions for developing people were to exist in society. I caught a strong equalitarian commitment from my father. ... I found myself in the Thirties orienting toward radical changes in the capitalistic economy but with an equally strong commitment to the maintenance and extension of democratic values in society. My study of Marxism and my contact with Marxists of various shades of opinion both in Michigan and New York deepened my understanding of the barriers to the extension of industrial democracy.[22]

---

20. Bradford, *National Training Laboratories*, 33. Bradford cites back to "Lippitt, R. *Training in Community Relations.* New York: Harper & Bros., 1949. 7."
21. Bradford, *National Training Laboratories*, 13 and 16.
22. Bradford, *National Training Laboratories*, 14–15.

Benne was also heavily influenced by sociologist Karl Mannheim. Although Mannheim was at odds with Marxism and the Frankfurt School in some areas of theory, he was heavily influenced by Marx and held similar beliefs to what would come to be associated with the Frankfurt School and "cultural Marxism." Mannheim, referring to his native Hungary, "rejected a materialist Marxist critique of this society. Hungary was to be changed by a spiritual renewal led by those who had reached a significant level of cultural awareness."[23] Much of NTL's efforts were focused on creating such cultural awareness.

Despite the ideological bent of its members, the Connecticut workshop was not a particularly radical endeavor. With its focus on anti-discrimination, it had little in common ideologically with Carmichael's black nationalism, and much more in common with what would become the mainstream civil rights movement of Martin Luther King Jr. It would be more revolutionary in the invention of the "T-Group," short for "training group." T-Groups, which would become the major tool of NTL, were a type of "experience-based learning" in which "participants work together in a small group over an extended period of time, learning through analysis of their own experiences, including feelings, reactions, perceptions, and behavior."[24] (T-Groups were also called basic skills training groups, laboratory training, encounter groups, sensitivity training, and human relations training.) [25]

The groups were also used as a research tool to study group dynamics, hence the "L" in NTL standing for "Laboratory/Laboratories." Training and research were seen as two parts of the same process to "develop effective methods of planned

---

23. Longhurst, *Karl Mannheim and the Contemporary Sociology of Knowledge.*
24. NTL Institute. "What is Sensitivity Training?"
25. Crosby, "T-group as Cutting Edge."
    Bradford, *National Training Laboratories*, Appendix 255.

change."[26] Lewin and team's techniques in the Connecticut workshop were overwhelmingly successful in causing trainees to change their behavior; every trainee reported undertaking new activities after the workshop, with those who had been measured as being more influential in their communities becoming even more active.[27]

At the beginning, T-Groups were very unstructured, with participants being free to move a group's agenda and activities in many directions; but over time, sensitivity training began to feature more active leaders.[28] In a T-Group, various group exercises including role-playing are performed for the purpose of helping the group to learn about interpersonal situations so that they can deal with such situations when they arise back home outside the group. T-Groups could serve as a tool to structure discussions to help groups make decisions, although some trainers came to oppose "cognitive input," preferring that participants open up exclusively about their emotions or operate nonverbally through "body movement and awareness methods."[29]

Shortly after Lewin's death, Lippitt, Bradford, and Benne founded the National Training Laboratory in Group Development.[30] In addition to Lewin's grant from the Office of Naval Research, NTL received its initial funding from the NEA, where Bradford was still working.[31] Just two years later in 1949,

---

26. Hirsch, "A History of the NTL Institute for Applied Behavioral Science," 58.

27. Harding, "Review of the book *Training in Community Relations*," 783.

28. Bradford, *National Training Laboratories*, 65.

29. Bradford, *National Training Laboratories*, 72 and 126.

30. NTL has had two naming revisions since its founding. It started in 1947 as the "National Training Laboratory in Group Development." Its name was then shortened to the "National Training Laboratories" in 1954. It was finally renamed the "NTL Institute for Applied Behavioral Science" in 1969. Hirsch, "A History of the NTL Institute for Applied Behavioral Science," 1.

31. Hirsch, "A History of the NTL Institute for Applied Behavioral Science," 26.

NTL became part of the NEA and began to receive major funding from the Carnegie Corporation foundation.[32] Expanding the work that the Connecticut workshop had started, NTL was conceived of as "an educational or re-educational or resocialization program directed first toward adult leaders with the goal of helping them become better group leaders and members, sensitive to the dynamic forces in groups and in themselves, and more competent agents of change in their roles and organizations."[33]

NTL also had a heavy research component, using T-Groups and other group methods to run experiments in what they called "action research," meaning "the scientific study of controlled social change."[34] NTL sought to "get and maintain encounters among the research-minded, the training-minded, the action-minded, and the value orientation-minded."[35] NTL's headquarters in Bethel, Maine, was an isolated live-in facility, aligned with Lewin's idea that "change could more readily occur if the person or persons were for a time on a type of 'Cultural Island' where back-home forces were less strong and change could more readily occur."[36]

Due to Lewin's study of change, training "agents of change" was core to NTL's mission. It defined a change-agent as one who attempts "to influence other people, to recognize their needs for change, to diagnose these needs in terms of what action is required to meet action, to evaluate the results of action according to plan, to replan, and finally to become independent of the particular

---

32. Bradford, *National Training Laboratories*, 66.
33. Bradford, *National Training Laboratories*, 5.
34. Harding, "Review of the book *Training in Community Relations*."
    Bradford, *National Training Laboratories*, Appendix 94.
35. Bradford, *National Training Laboratories*, 20 and 47.
36. Bradford, *National Training Laboratories*, 44.

'outside' consultant on training help who may have been required at the first stages of the training or re-training process." [37]

NTL studied how to change people's ideologies and ran groups specifically designed to help people learn to achieve policy change.[38] One of the first papers produced by NTL was "The Change-Agent Skills," which included:

- "Determining the barriers, the resistance, the degree of readiness to change"
- "Making changees aware of the need for change" including through tools of "shock" and "guilt"
- "Creating a feeling of responsibility to engage in this change by active personal participation"
- "Making catharsis possible"
- "Skill in dealing wisely with changees' ideology, myths, traditions, [and] values"
- "Understanding stress on changees' beliefs and behavior"
- "continuing, spreading, [and] maintaining" the change.[39]

NTL was deeply aware of how change in groups occurred. It studied people's "influenceability," "ability to influence others," "the effect of group pressure toward uniformity," and the emergence of group standards. NTL understood that in order to create change, "detecting and correcting fallacies in group thinking" was necessary and that "member ideologies" must be integrated into "common group traditions, ideology, and goals."[40] NTL found that to have groups see what their needs are, "regardless of their own interest,"

37. Bradford, *National Training Laboratories*, Appendix 91.
38. Bradford, *National Training Laboratories*, 95 and Appendix 37.
39. Bradford, *National Training Laboratories*, 39–41.
40. Bradford, *National Training Laboratories*, 42, 121 and Appendix 14, 265.

one needed to find change-agents who could "move freely across social lines."[41] It also understood that "language usage rigidity," meaning being too strict about the definitions of words, was a barrier to group communication.[42]

The 1967 book *Concepts for Social Change*, funded by the US Department of Education, described the process of societal change as follows:

 During the life of a typical innovation or change-enterprise, perceived resistance moves through a cycle. In the *early stage*, when only a few pioneer thinkers take the reform seriously, resistance appears massive and undifferentiated. "Everyone" knows better: "no one in his right mind" could advocate the change. Proponents are labeled crackpots and visionaries.

In the *second stage*, when the movement for change has begun to grow, the forces pro and con become identifiable. The opposition can be defined by its position in the social system, and its power can be appraised.

Direct conflict and a showdown mark the *third stage*, as resistance becomes mobilized to crush the upstart proposal. Enthusiastic supporters of a new idea have frequently underestimated the strength of their opponents. ...

The *fourth stage*, after the decisive battles, finds supporters of the change in power. The persisting

41. Bradford, *National Training Laboratories*, Appendix 142–143.
42. Bradford, *National Training Laboratories*, 62.

resistance is, at this stage, seen as a stubborn hidebound, cantankerous nuisance. ...

In a *fifth stage*, the old adversaries are as few, and as alienated, as were the advocates in the first stage.[43]

Accordingly, the core element for a change-agent to overcome is resistance. NTL studied various forms of resistance, which included:

- "dependence" on their parent's views including on "such basic items as language, religion, politics, childrearing, and what a school should do"
- the "superego" leading people to believe that social change could result in "utter chaos" (with the phrase "better dead than Red!" cited as an example of such resistance)
- internalizing the responsibility for negative outcomes in their lives instead of laying "the blame for their predicament on faulty social mechanisms"
- "regression" to "tried-and-true fundamentals" at times when they allegedly should "experiment with new approaches."[44]

NTL had also understood that "ideological conflicts," including rejecting an idea by thinking "only Communists act that way," were a source of resistance.[45] On the social system level, reasons for

---

43. Cooperative Project for Educational Development, *Concepts for Social Change*, 11–12.

    Paragraph breaks added for readability

44. Cooperative Project for Educational Development, *Concepts for Social Change*, 14–18.

45. Bradford, *National Training Laboratories*, Appendix 39–40.

resistance included "conformity to norms," "vested interests" (with taxpayer resistance to social programs given as an example), "the sacrosanct," and rejection of those labeled as "outside agitators" or "Communists."[46]

To overcome the various forms of resistance, NTL found resistance would be decreased if changees:

- developed "their own understanding of the need for the change and an explicit awareness of how they feel about it and what can be done about these feelings"
- "accept (internalize) the desired change as an alternative to the resistance system which may already be established. In other words the conflict must be internalized in order to release problem solving activity."[47]
- "if [participants] feel that the project is their own—not one devised and operated by outsiders"
- "if the project clearly has whole hearted support from top officials of the system"
- "if the project accords with values and ideals that have long been acknowledged by participants"
- "if participants have joined in diagnostic efforts leading them to agree on the basic problem and to feel its importance"
- "if it is recognized that innovations are likely to be misunderstood and misinterpreted"
- "if participants experience acceptance, support, trust, and confidence in their relations with one another"

---

46. Cooperative Project for Educational Development, *Concepts for Social Change*, 18–22.

47. Bradford, *National Training Laboratories*, Appendix 194.

- can be made to "no longer look nostalgically at a Golden Age in the past but anticipate their Utopia in the days to come."[48]

All of those tactics would become recognizable in the Racism Awareness Trainings to follow.

NTL also understood the challenges that newly developed change-agents would face in spreading their change at home:

> The delegate who returns to his home situation and who seeks immediately to introduce changes without recognition that the changes he proposes are likely to be met with resistance because they require actions that are different from those authorized by established tradition is likely to find his efforts frustrated. In seeking to innovate changes he can easily be cast in the deviant role and meet with rejection. One alternative demonstrated by the Merei experiment is that of introducing changes slowly so that fundamental shifts from already established standards are not required and so that step-by-step modifications resulting in changed behavior can occur.[49]

While at first glance this may all appear innately manipulative and wrong, it's important to understand the wide range of contexts in which NTL was working. Lewin's theory of change originally gained attention in part due to his study of diet habits, where making people aware of the necessity of change and overcoming resistance is

---

48. Cooperative Project for Educational Development, *Concepts for Social Change*, 22–23.
49. Bradford, *National Training Laboratories*, Appendix 269.

unobjectionable.[50] According to Benne, "the generalized notion of a change-agent cut across various roles of social practice, whether in social work, education, action leadership, and management."[51] Much of NTL's work was in the field of "organization development," and many of the change-agents NTL sought to create were managers in workplaces who would simply try to create change to help employees get along better and be more productive. One of the more moderate definitions of "planned change" that NTL used in this context was "helping managers and administrators improve the effectiveness of their organizations."[52] To NTL's credit, it understood that resistance to change could often be rational and desirable, devoting a whole chapter in *Concepts for Social Change* to describing many ways in which this could be the case and arguing that it is important "for those seeking change to consider the costs of ignoring, overriding, or dismissing as irrational those who emerge as their opponents."[53]

While sensitivity trainings would increasingly become more blatantly manipulative as time went on (regardless of whether or not the trainers acknowledged manipulation), materials from NTL's first year of existence (1947) stated:

 The concept of the change agent is not one of manipulation. Change is produced through people's own efforts, not through manipulation. In the ideology used in this discussion of the change agent, he involves

50. Stanford SPARQ, "To Make Change, Start with a Crowd."

51. Bradford, *National Training Laboratories*, 20.

52. Cooperative Project for Educational Development, *Concepts for Social Change*, 1.

53. Cooperative Project for Educational Development, *Concepts for Social Change*, 26–36.

all people in planning and discussing the changes, not in secret introduction of changes."[54]

Theoretically, according to Benne, "democratic group deliberation thus gives 'free' thought a high place in its scheme of values as the best basis on which intelligent action can be based," although he also believed that democratic groups "must develop intolerance of such factors as: non-influenceability on the part of members of the group, refusal to consider alternative solutions to problems, refusal to face facts."[55]

Fundamentally, T-Groups and change-agentry are simply tools. Like a knife, they can be used for good or for bad; to slice food or stab. For Benne, this tool worked well to advance his ideas of democratic socialism. Benne argued:

in a society which could no longer rely upon common historical traditions to guide it, men would have to learn a process of planning their future ... working out new orientations, new common orientations, and planning processes require that a social process be re-educative. It needs to be re-educative because men

---

54. Bradford, *National Training Laboratories*, Appendix 133.

Sensitivity training in schools was heavily criticized. Sensitivity training for students sparked a political fight in Orange County, California. U.S. Congress, *Congressional Record* H15324 (June 10, 1969). A professor of science education and critic of sensitivity training in schools noted it "deteriorated" working relationships between teachers, "increased alienation ... between school officials and community members," "increase[d] rather than decrease[d] the defensiveness of associates," caused "disillusionment and value disintegration," and that while in some situations sensitivity training could provide "useful knowledge and experiences," in general it could "be more damaging than helpful." Edwards, "Sensitivity Training and Education." Author as a "professor of science education" from Edwards, *Educational Change*.

55. Bradford, *National Training Laboratories*, 43.

must somehow, through encounter with one another, work out ways of changing their normative principles and their policies toward commonly accepted and acceptable orientations. And this calls for re-education, not alone on the level of information and motoric skill, although these are important too, but at the level of value orientation.[56]

NTL staff understood their power. A staff member told Bradford, "you're now in a position where you can form ideology for other people."[57] As a critic of T-Groups noted in 1963, "because the T-Group is the major source of reinforcement, and their values are mixed, then the reinforcement of emitted behavior is just as likely to be for the wrong things as the right things."[58]

However, the vast majority of NTL's work in the late 1940s and throughout the 1950s did not appear ideologically objectionable, although it's unclear what impact it might have had beyond the trainings NTL conducted. For example, NTL studied how to successfully communicate "a body of social science theory to a learning group." It's easy to imagine how the same unobjectionable research used to help teach a valid social science theory could be used to teach a radical politicized one.[59] But another study NTL conducted related to improving parent-teen communication, which appears to be a thoroughly valid cause.[60] Going back to the Connecticut anti-discrimination workshop, Benne saw his change-agents' "generalized strategies of action and approaches to help bring about changes in attitudes and behavior beyond the anti-

---

56. Bradford, *National Training Laboratories*, 14.
57. Bradford, *National Training Laboratories*, Appendix 178.
58. Ordiorne, "The Trouble with Sensitivity Training," 13.
59. Bradford, *National Training Laboratories*, 109.
60. Bradford, *National Training Laboratories*, 107.

discriminatory context to other enterprises in education, in business, and in the life of the church."[61]

Nevertheless, Benne had internal battles at NTL. He was unhappy that new staff weren't sufficiently focused on "social action or broader social change," and that they failed to match his "social radicalism."[62] Another staffer who came to NTL as a "political activist" also expressed frustration regarding its increasing focus on "personal growth."[63]

NTL's impact spread at a seemingly exponential rate. As early as 1948, NTL became known across the country and was the focus of both favorable and unfavorable magazine and newspaper articles in the 1950s. By the late 1950s, it was widely known internationally.[64] As recognition grew, so did the research staff. Staff came to NTL's programs each year from major universities across the nation including Harvard, Yale, and UC Berkeley.[65] In 1949, it began to form the NTL "Network" to maintain connections with the people who attended their programs. Speaking of the Network, Bradford noted, "we looked always for those who would influence others, and in that sense we infiltrated a wide variety of groups and occupations."[66]

By 1957, "1,500 persons had come to Bethel from all but three states, all the territories, and 33 foreign countries."[67] By 1960 they were conducting over 20 training laboratories annually and enrolling approximately 2,000 adult leaders.[68] A scholar of NTL's

---

61. Bradford, *National Training Laboratories*, 19.
62. Bradford, *National Training Laboratories*, 21.
63. Hirsch, "A History of the NTL Institute for Applied Behavioral Science," 56–57.
64. Bradford, *National Training Laboratories*, 52 and 73.
65. Bradford, *National Training Laboratories*, 56.
66. Bradford, *National Training Laboratories*, 64.
67. Bradford, *National Training Laboratories*, 106.
68. Bradford, *National Training Laboratories*, 131.

history wrote that by the late 1960s, "NTL assumed an almost mythical status as an agent of the new order."[69]

In 1974, Bradford estimated "it would be a conservative figure to say that at least twenty to thirty million persons have been touched by group experiences that had some relationship, usually unknown to them, to NTL."[70] Throughout the 1950s and 1960s, NTL's work inspired the founding of new laboratories performing similar work.[71] Sensitivity training gained wide adoption in industry; NTL received a grant from IBM and conducted trainings for staff from Bell Telephone, General Electric, and many other corporations. Sensitivity training gained acceptance among churches, with NTL working frequently with the National Council of Churches and forming particularly close ties with Protestant churches.[72]

Sensitivity training also was adopted within non-profit organizations, with NTL working directly with the American Red Cross and the American Cancer Society. NTL methods also influenced the YMCA and schools. Having been a part of the NEA until becoming an independent organization in 1966, and maintaining a close relationship even after their split, NTL had wide reach into primary and secondary school systems, and also into higher education.[73] Bradford estimated that "more than 15,000

---

69. Hirsch, "A History of the NTL Institute for Applied Behavioral Science," 4.
70. Bradford, *National Training Laboratories*, 203.
71. Bradford, *National Training Laboratories*, 98 and 207.
72. Bradford, *National Training Laboratories*, 123–124, 131, 151, and 203–204.
73. Year of NTL split with NEA from Bradford, *National Training Laboratories*, 168.
  Sensitivity training in schools was heavily criticized. Sensitivity training for students sparked a political fight in Orange County, California. U.S. Congress, *Congressional Record* H15324 (June 10, 1969). An academic professor of science education and critic of sensitivity training in schools noted it "deteriorated" working relationships between teachers, "increased alienation ... between school officials and community members", "increase rather than decrease the defensiveness of associates",

students and faculty" attended their Higher Education Laboratories, and NTL had infiltrated the teaching community "in a variety of departments in many universities through the number of university faculty members who joined the staff on NTL programs."[74]

NTL reached deeply into the federal government, particularly through its programs with the State Department, but also through the National Institute of Mental Health, the US Office of Education, the National Science Foundation, the US Public Health Service, the Bureau of the Budget, the National Security Agency, and several branches of the military.[75] But NTL's impact extended beyond the United States, training people and inspiring programs on every continent except Antarctica.[76]

NTL's global impact is especially alarming considering that NTL, even from its early days, has been controversial. The fields of social work, psychiatry, education, and much of psychology remained "generally hostile" throughout the 1950s. Bradford recalled fellow adult educators telling him "unless I gave up NTL what reputation I had would be lost and I would never achieve anything." Despite NTL being a part of the NEA, Bradford felt ostracized even there.[77] Perhaps most dramatically, Bradford recalled a training he was set to run at a UNESCO conference in the spring of 1948:

 At the St. Francis Hotel, on the day before the

---

caused "disillusionment and value disintegration", and that while in some situations sensitivity training could provide "useful knowledge and experiences" in general it could "be more damaging than helpful." Edwards, "Sensitivity Training and Education." Author as a "professor of science education" from Edwards, *Educational Change.*

74. Bradford, *National Training Laboratories*, 206.
75. Bradford, *National Training Laboratories*, 206–207 and Appendix 304, 334.
76. Bradford, *National Training Laboratories*, 118 and 212–221.
77. Bradford, *National Training Laboratories*, 73.

meeting, about 150 persons, including college presidents, movie stars, and others of renown, were gathered to be "trained" for their roles. I had met at lunch the day before with the president of a California college who was to introduce me the following day. I was aware of his hostility, but naively put it down to the fact that my reputation was very much less than his. The next day, with only the two of us on the stage, he made a short statement to the effect that he did not believe in group dynamics and was not going to introduce me. He then walked off the stage. I have seldom felt more lonesome. The tension in the audience rose.[78]

While the source of the California college president's hostility was not specified, it was perhaps not surprising. From its founding in 1947, NTL was aware that its programs "created various degrees of stress for some individuals and we needed either a psychiatrist or clinical psychologist present." In 1949, psychiatric staff brought into NTL, while very friendly to the organization, reported that "some casualties are probably inevitable and the psychiatrist is a wise safeguard."[79]

The risk of "casualties" grew worse as time went on. At a training in 1950, a riot almost broke out due to conflict in a T-Group.[80] As of 1953, NTL noticed some participants were leaving T-Groups with "emotional disturbances" and served "as a bad advertisement for the lab."[81] Although exceedingly rare as a proportion of participants in NTL's programs, by the mid-1960s its

---

78. Bradford, *National Training Laboratories*, 51.
79. Bradford, *National Training Laboratories*, Appendix 209.
80. Bradford, *National Training Laboratories*, 68.
81. Bradford, *National Training Laboratories*, 238.

trainings triggered at least four people with previous psychiatric histories to have "psychotic episodes and become seriously ill."[82] Despite these incidents, by the late 1960s, the number of "psychologically disturbed persons" participating in training was increasing, and NTL's trainers were not prepared to deal with their pathologies.[83] In 1970, NTL settled a lawsuit after a delegate to a management lab committed suicide.[84]

In 1969 the American Psychiatric Association assigned a task force to study the issue. In 1971, psychiatrists at Stanford and the University of Chicago, one of whom chaired the American Psychiatric Association's task force, published "Study of Encounter Group Casualties," in which they found that 9.4 percent—a "conservative estimate"—of their 170 subjects who completed NTL's programs could be counted as casualties. A casualty was defined as "an individual who, as a direct result of his experience in the encounter group, became more psychologically distressed or employed more maladaptive mechanisms of defence, or both; furthermore this negative change was not a transient but an enduring one, as judged eight months after the group experience."[85]

Three of the casualties they studied had "psychotic decompositions," including manic psychosis and schizophrenia. Several of the casualties had "depressive or anxiety symptoms, or both, ranging from low grade tension or discouragement to severe crippling anxiety attacks to a major six-month depression with a 40-lb weight loss and suicidal ideation." One casualty committed suicide. Several more casualties "noted a deterioration of their interpersonal life; they withdrew or avoided others, experienced more distrust, were less willing to reach out or to take risks with

82. Mann, "Sensitivity Training," 45.
83. Lakin, "Some Ethical Issues in Sensitivity Training," 924.
84. Bradford, *National Training Laboratories*, 191.
85. Yalom and Lieberman, "A Study of Encounter Group Casualties," 17–19 and 28.

others." One of those casualties was part of an encounter group discussing racial issues. Their study also found that it was "three times more likely that a subject who is in an encounter group will seek psycho-therapy during the time he is in the group, or in the eight-month follow-up period, than a control subject."[86]

By 1971, however, several different organizations were running encounter groups, and they had developed substantially from the early T-Groups NTL ran in the 1940s and 1950s. The 1971 study included groups run by NTL, and some of the casualties in their findings were produced by NTL, but groups run by the Esalen Institute and Synanon produced a greater rate of casualties.

Bradford wrote:

> There is no question that Esalen and the Growth Centers around the country have been influenced to some extent by NTL and the laboratory method. ... While the Encounter Movement is much more intra- and interpersonally oriented than the early developments of NTL and the organization development trend, it nevertheless owes much of its genesis to NTL.[87]

The Esalen Institute spun off from NTL in 1962. It became a core pillar of the 1960s "Human Potential Movement" (NTL was also a part of the movement), which "attempted to fuse Marx with Freud" and blamed contemporary society for having "overly repressive socialization mechanisms."[88] Affiliated with psychologist Carl Rogers, who also worked with NTL, Esalen and Rogers

---

86. Yalom and Lieberman, "A Study of Encounter Group Casualties," 19 and 24.
87. Bradford, *National Training Laboratories*, 207.
88. Founding date from Callahan, "A History of the Esalen Institute." All else from Hirsch, "A History of the NTL Institute for Applied Behavioral Science," 122.

adjusted the tools NTL developed to function more like group therapy.[89] Rogers famously wrote:

> sensitivity training is perhaps the most significant social invention of this century. The demand for it is utterly beyond belief. It is one of the most rapidly growing social phenomena in the United States. It has permeated industry, is coming into education, is reaching families, professionals in the helping fields and many other individuals.[90]

Esalen experimented with more extreme forms of encounter groups, including nude sessions.[91] Esalen's style led to fierce opposition to sensitivity training from the leadership of the Church of Jesus Christ of Latter-day Saints, which created negative repercussions for NTL's operations in Utah.[92]

Synanon, founded in 1958, originally marketed itself as an organization, similar to Alcoholics Anonymous, that rehabilitated people with all different types of drug addictions. Originally perceived very positively by the general public, Synanon was the basis of a 1965 feature film of the same name that focused on how the group cured members of their addictions.[93] However, Synanon's founder, Charles E. Dederich, decided early on that:

> treating addicts was merely a byproduct of his larger mission. He wanted to create an experimental society

---

89. For an example of how Rogers ran such groups, watch the film *A Journey into Self*: McGraw, *A Journey into Self*.

90. Bradford, *National Training Laboratories*, Appendix 3, 207.

91. U.S. Congress, *Congressional Record*, H15327 (June 10, 1969).

92. Bradford, *National Training Laboratories*, 178 and 209.

93. Quince, *Synanon*.

that would transform the world. ... its goal was no less than a utopian revolution. Synanon was a new way of living, as important to its members as any of the world's major religions.

Synanon rejected all pharmaceuticals or tapering drugs to get addicts clean. Instead, their main method of treatment was called "The Game" and was directly built on NTL's group dynamics tools to create change in resistant individuals. In The Game:

> people sat in a circle to express (and often shout) their frustrations at each other. The confrontational approach was a way to hash out everything that bothered you about others in your group. It was supposed to help you learn about yourself as well. While playing the Game, your frustrations didn't even need to be true. Lying was just one of many strategies in The Game, which could last anywhere from one to 48 hours.

In 1974, Synanon followed the same path as Scientology and decided to seek IRS recognition as a religious organization.[94] By the mid-1970s, all Synanon members were forced to shave their heads, and some members were forced to have vasectomies, abortions, and divorces. Synanon members:

> viciously beat a trucker in Badger, California on November 11, 1977, after a road rage incident in which the trucker supposedly cut off a car full of Synanites on the highway. Dederich reportedly

_____

94. Novak, "Synanon's Sober Utopia."

shamed the four Synanon men involved for not physically attacking the trucker in retaliation. They remedied the situation by roaming the town with guns looking for the man, who turned out to be a guy named Ron Eidsen.

Once they found Eidsen, the group pistol-whipped him to a pulp in his own front yard, screaming that they were going to kill him. Eidsen's wife and five children could only watch on in horror. The Synanite thugs threatened to come back for his family if he ever messed with the cult again.

By 1978 Synanon had $300,000 worth of weapons and had "periodically beaten ranchers in Marin County with property adjacent to their headquarters." Synanon participated in multiple attempted murders as well. Synanon had compounds in both Marin County and Los Angeles, where they had considerable influence with local government, which often prevented police investigations. They did, however, lose a $300,000 lawsuit for causing psychosis in one of their members who had gone to Synanon seeking treatment for depression, paranoia, and marijuana use. After that incident, Synanon became "only interested in die-hard devotees who could actively contribute to their warped community in some way." Despite these events, Synanon maintained ties with major corporations including IBM and Heinz until the 1980s. Synanon was finally shut down in 1991 for financial reasons after facing issues with the IRS.[95]

While Synanon does not represent how NTL ran its training groups, it does demonstrate the power of the techniques first developed at NTL and how they could produce extremely harmful

---

95. Novak, "The Man Who Fought the Synanon Cult and Won."

repercussions when used for ill purposes. NTL knew people might gain interest in their study of group dynamics for malicious reasons, yet they didn't seem to care: "It is irrelevant whether the personal motivation for this understanding is 'intellectual curiosity,' 'desire to solve social problems' or 'personal obsession with power.'"[96]

In the late 1960s, sensitivity training and NTL became a focus of political controversy.[97] In April 1968, one letter from the conservative Network of Patriotic Letter Writers, which was entered into the congressional record, alleged that sensitivity training was analogous to the coerced "self-criticism" techniques used by communist regimes to enforce compliance (a.k.a. "struggle sessions").[98] While perhaps conflating NTL's methods with methods used by other groups, the similarity between some training groups and communist struggle sessions is indeed striking, as The Game at Synanon demonstrates.

By June 1969, the political controversy had grown, with 12 pages of collated materials criticizing sensitivity training entered into the congressional record. One paper found:

 A study of logs of numerous sensitivity or T-Group training sessions would lead one to believe that the promoters of these programs are trying to homogenize the members of the group. Individualism must be sacrificed. ... Since very few people have taken the time to construct a complete brief and thereby justify their various beliefs, such a procedure tends to destroy even the shallow roots which the individual may have developed. If this happens, then he commences to feel

96. Bradford, *National Training Laboratories*, Appendix 292.
97. Batista, "If you're interested in T-groups."
98. U.S. Congress, *Congressional Record*, H10433–H10435 (April 24, 1968).

very dependent upon the group. He begins seeking 'consensus' before he dares take a position. Approval can become more important to him than truth.

Another similarly detailed the "methods used in training":

The learner is involved in the training situation to a point where he feels it vital to become an accepted member of the group and to help work out group problems. An attempt is made to develop an atmosphere of permissiveness in which it is possible for individuals to examine their own behavior, ideas, motives, and values, and to accept criticism from others without defensiveness. Group standards are developed which give rewards to an individual as he changes his actions from less to more group-centered behavior. Opportunities are created for each learner to test and practice "new," "improved," and "appropriate" behavior.

Anxieties: Participants can become easily aroused in the training situation for several reasons ... It becomes the duty of the trainer to dispel these anxieties without making it easy for the trainee to escape from the change process. Proponents maintain this is one of the most crucial points of training ...

The role of trainer: The role of the trainer is a complex one. He is an initiator, agenda planner, mediator, a source of new values, behavior model, and a facilitator of the learning process. The trainer has no alternative but to manipulate; his job is to plan and produce behavior in order to create changes in other people.

Multiple papers noted the similarities between sensitivity training and psychological warfare techniques used against American prisoners during the Korean War. Another document included a mother recounting her son's story:

> My son is 17. Last night he returned from church in tears. He had attended an "encounter group" meeting for "sensitivity training." The members meet twice a week. They pick a victim for each meeting. Then the members tell him what they don't like about him. My son's friends criticized his manners, haircut, eye color, acne scars, intelligence, vocational plans, clothes, car, and even his parents. They were brutal and extremely unfair. An assistant minister leads the group. He has had no training in counseling or psychology. The man publicly called my son "chicken," for getting upset.

The records ended by summarizing:

> In spite of the claimed goals of Sensitivity Training, which are love, trust, openness of communication, leadership and a better understanding of others, these programs have been proven to cause distrust and the breakdown of communication between participants. ... Proponents claim that "Sensitivity Training is a means to alter the basic personality structure of an individual". Participants are manipulated by group pressure and by the scientific technique of the trainer, whose job is to plan and produce behavior in order to create changes in other people.[99]

---

99. U.S. Congress, *Congressional Record*, H15322–H15335 (June 10, 1969).

The field of sensitivity training was not a monolith. There were good as well as bad trainings, with many of the bad ones run by "enthusiastic amateurs" with severely limited experience.[100] What is clear, however, is that the techniques NTL developed were at times used negligently and/or for negative purposes. Saul Alinsky, the famed author of "Rules for Radicals," built off Lewin's work.[101]

While the field of Racism Awareness Training as developed by Robert Terry, Pat Bidol, and others is not as actively malicious as, for example, Synanon, it nonetheless adopted and built on the group dynamics tools NTL developed to convince, pressure, and/or manipulate people into changing their views and values. Either NTL's ties to industry or churches could explain how they came to the attention of DIM. We know NTL's methods deeply influenced Terry because he frequently used NTL's "change-agent" language and regularly cited "organizational development consultant" Warren Bennis in his writings, including quoting Bennis as saying:

> Using himself [the consultant], most of all, he aims to detect and get close to the important "data" to exploit every encounter he can in order to help the client-system see "reality". He uses situations, as they develop spontaneously, to work through the tensions and resistances associated with them. Most of all, he uses <u>himself</u> as a <u>role model</u>. ... To the extent that this role model is emulated ... change can occur[102]

Bennis had worked with NTL beginning at least as early as 1955, helping to run its summer sessions.[103] During the 1959–1960

---

100. Edwards, "Sensitivity Training and Education," 259.
101. Daniels, "Kurt Lewin Notes."
102. Terry, "Action from the Boundary." 247.
103. Bradford, *National Training Laboratories*, 97.

academic year, Bennis became adjunct staff.[104] In 1962, he was added to the board.[105] Finally, in 1969, Bennis became "far and away the first choice of almost everyone" to replace Leland Bradford as NTL's president.[106] Bennis accepted the position and planned to create an NTL "International University for Social Change" intended "to work on utopias and how you build new communities," to "really reach into government," and to expand programming on "cross cultural relation" and "racism."[107] Bennis thought that he was living in "a revolutionary period in our country's history" and that NTL should become:

> the center for social change in our society—the place where people come to decide what kind of society we should have and how to achieve it. It should be eminent, radical, experimental, central. It must be radically conceived and radically sold. If it is not defined this way from the very beginning it will be defined as a place where this cannot happen—as a place where the only thing that happens is that people learn to patch up organizations, as a place where the only people there are people who are only interested in short-run change. If it is to be real it must include radicals on some basis.[108]

While Bennis would ultimately back out of the position for personal reasons, and the university would never come to fruition, much of what he desired NTL to become was already underway.

---

104. Bradford, *National Training Laboratories*, 135.
105. Bradford, *National Training Laboratories*, 153.
106. Bradford, *National Training Laboratories*, 183.
107. Bradford, *National Training Laboratories*, Appendix 342.
108. Bradford, *National Training Laboratories*, Appendix 345-346.

During the 1960s, NTL, which had worked on race issues since its founding, "faced a confrontation ... on the black-white issue" and came to believe "social rebuilding" was necessary to fix "interracial tensions."[109] An academic critic of sensitivity training noted that trainers were conducting "confrontation sessions" consisting "of contrived racial encounters where whites and blacks openly confront one another."[110] In 1968, a "Black Caucus," formed at NTL's Bethel campus, presented non-negotiable demands to Bradford. He talked them into negotiating, but ultimately agreed to many of their requests, which included the creation of a separate exclusively-black intern program, a "special category in NTL's network for Black Trainers," and affirmative action to achieve a goal of 20 percent black representation in various NTL programs (even though African Americans made up only approximately 11 percent of the US population at the time).[111] In 1969, NTL began "a program on race relations for city managers" and started a well-funded Black Affairs Center.[112] In the late 1960s NTL's programs were increasingly populated by political and cultural radicals of many types, and NTL generally "tended to follow the dictates of cultural radicals."[113]

Beyond racial conflict, a "Women's Caucus" formed to attack "male privilege" at NTL. Edith Seashore, the woman who led that attack, later became the president of NTL in the 1970s.[114] Under her leadership, NTL's board was reconstituted to cap the

---

109. Bradford, *National Training Laboratories*, 129 and 132.
110. Edwards, "Sensitivity Training and Education," 258.
111. Bradford, *National Training Laboratories*, 181 and 183.
  U.S. Census Bureau, *A Look at the 1940 Census*.
112. Bradford, *National Training Laboratories*, 187–188.
113. Hirsch, "A History of the NTL Institute for Applied Behavioral Science," 84–85.
114. Hirsch, "A History of the NTL Institute for Applied Behavioral Science," 87 and 104.

representation of white males at one-third of the board seats.[115] Right before his retirement, Bradford was "accused by younger members of being part of an 'old guard' that impeded progress."[116]

The NTL Institute for Applied Behavioral Science continues to exist, and it considers "social justice" its "first value," seeking to "raise greater consciousness about white privilege" and the "dismantling of the laws, culture, and institutions that allow racism to thrive."[117] NTL opposed President Trump's September 2020 executive order banning so-called diversity training in government agencies that suggest "either (1) that the United States is an inherently racist or evil country or (2) that any race or ethnicity is inherently racist or evil." NTL currently conducts such "diversity and equity trainings."[118] NTL wrote:

> Too many of us have been educated in a system which overlooks the racist origins and present realities of systemic racism, understanding it only as individual acts of overt hatred. Many scholars have worked to prove a more accurate representation of the history of the United States.[119]

Such "scholars" include Pat Bidol, who has been an NTL member since 1973, and would become the "dean and facilitator" of their Human Interaction Labs.[120] In fact, multiple key figures in the

115. Hirsch, "A History of the NTL Institute for Applied Behavioral Science," 105.
116. Hirsch, "A History of the NTL Institute for Applied Behavioral Science," 86.
117. NTL Institute, "Responding to Systemic Racism."
118. Vought, "Training in the Federal Government."
119. NTL Institute, "Responding to President Trump's Memo on Diversity Training."
120. Bidol, Linkedin.
   American University. "Patricia Bidol-Padva Bio."

spread of the "Power + Prejudice" definition of racism and Racism Awareness Training would hold leadership positions at NTL.[121]

In 1974 after his retirement from NTL, Leland Bradford wrote:

> I venture to predict that the very concept of education will gradually change in elementary and secondary education, and hopefully both, particularly in adult education. Many organizations in many occupations are even presently undergoing review and renewal that encompass a very different concept of worker and manager than existed in the past. And it is not so difficult to predict that the present social turmoil in the world will be aided in resolution by the concepts of involvement and joint collaboration of researchers, professional teachers, practitioners, and people, which has long been one of the basic concepts of NTL.[122]

He was wrong that the concepts NTL developed would aid in the resolution of social turmoil, but he was right they would take over education. Bradford added:

> H.G. Wells once wrote of a Utopia where 'our education is our law.' Some day people may be able to relate to themselves and others in such a fashion that a

---

121. The most notable is Judith Katz, discussed in Part 2, who served as a board member for the NTL Institute. Kaleel Jamison Consulting Group, "Judith H. Katz."

Another example is Beth Applegate, an NTL member who writes on intersectionality, white "anti-racism," and other social justice topics, and who is a co-chair of a chapter of the radical group Standing Up For Racial Justice. Applegate, "Member Mondays: Beth Applegate."

122. Bradford, *National Training Laboratories*, 222.

different social structure and accepted ethics can be viable.

Perhaps what NTL has striven toward will be helpful along the way.[123]

---

123. Bradford, *National Training Laboratories*, 224.

The Detroit Industrial Mission
Goes Radical

In 1967, two members of DIM leadership (Hugh White and Robert Batchelder) left to pursue new opportunities. (White was promoted to lead the National Committee for Industrial Mission.) New leadership took over, and new staff were hired. James Campbell became Executive Director. Jesse Christman, who wanted to bring about what he called a "Fourth Industrial Revolution" (essentially turning industry into socialist-style co-ops), became the "visionary" for DIM. One of the two new staff members hired in this period was Robert Terry.[1]

Terry was an ordained American Baptist Minister, a graduate of Cornell University and Colgate-Rochester Divinity School, and was working to obtain his PhD in divinity from the University of Chicago. Most of the information on DIM in this book draws from Terry's 1973 divinity dissertation, "Action from the Boundary: An Historical Study of Detroit Industrial Mission."[2] Despite Terry's

---

1. Terry, "Action from the Boundary," 273–276.
2. Terry, "Action from the Boundary."

theological background, DIM wanted to communicate in ways that did not require religious conviction. DIM realized that by focusing on spreading the value of "participation" into the ethic of large industrial organizations, it could "communicate to secular types as well as religious."[3]

DIM had slowly been moving in a more radical direction in the years before the riot, but July 1967 changed everything. DIM, with connections in the black militant community via the West Central Organization, started to do "switchboarding" (initiating or upon request serving as a go-between to get industry in contact with activists). In this same general period, DIM also helped raise a thousand dollars for East Side Voices for Independent Detroit, run by ultra-militant Frank Ditto.[4] When DIM heard about the New Detroit Committee, the staff sent a telegram to former Mission board member Joseph Hudson congratulating him on being appointed chairman, with copies sent to Governor Romney and Mayor Cavanaugh. That telegram asked for the committee to include "those normally overlooked or deliberately rejected" and "dissenters." Shortly after, DIM received a response from Hudson asking for recommendations of names. That led to Hudson's meeting with militants and the placement of radical voices on the New Detroit Committee.[5] However, DIM was disappointed that even after pressure to increase the number of militants on the committee, Hudson let on only three. Hugh White also helped Hudson prepare for New Detroit's first meetings, with White

---

3. Terry, "Action from the Boundary," 304. Terry as minister from Terry, "Action from the Boundary," 413.

4. Terry, "Action from the Boundary," 346.

5. Notably, Hudson explained to the militants in that meeting that "he was solely responsible for the selection of the membership to the committee and for determining the objectives and goals of the committee. He was not to be hampered by the governor or the mayor." Terry, "Action from the Boundary," 312–318.

suggesting to Hudson that "concessions will have to be made" both to and by the militants.[6]

Not long after the riots, Christman felt it was important DIM add a black staff member. DIM broadly felt the riots showed they needed to improve their "understanding and analysis of the racial condition in the United States and particularly Detroit."[7] Terry recalled:

> The decision to add a black man to the staff raised thorny issues as staff requirements and job description became problematic. How militant should a black man be? Should whites consider this an important criteria? How much should he want to get his identity in the black community rather than in the industrial mission? How prepared was the staff, being all white, to work effectively with a black man? How much should the Mission pay to attract a top, articulate, black spokesman with requisite skills for doing industrial mission?[8]

This neurosis over how DIM's white staff should feel about interacting with a black person, rather than simply hiring a black staff member and treating him like every other staff member, would persist throughout the Mission's operations and as Terry developed his racial philosophy. The staff eventually decided they wanted "an advocate of black power and a man conversant with the militant struggle for justice in America," and, on June 1, 1968, they hired their new black staff member, Douglas E. Fitch.

---

6. Terry, "Action from the Boundary," 320–322.
7. Terry, "Action from the Boundary," 326 and 344.
8. Terry, "Action from the Boundary," 382.

Fitch had been a pastor and social worker, but also a racial justice activist. He had once been president of an NAACP chapter. Like Stokely Carmichael, Fitch worked with Martin Luther King, Jr. in the early 1960s, but became substantially more radical over time. Immediately prior to joining DIM, he worked with the Black Congress of Los Angeles, a united front of Black Power organizations.[9] Multiple Black Panther factions were members of the Black Congress, with one including Angela Davis as an active member. Davis at the time was working on her PhD in philosophy under Frankfurt School philosopher Herbert Marcuse. She would later become nationally known for her ties to violent revolutionary groups and her work with Communist Party USA. Most Black Congress member organizations rejected integration and nonviolence, and the Black Congress organized a rally that featured Stokely Carmichael as a speaker.[10] Additionally, Fitch "established the first human relations council in San Bernardino County."[11] As "human relations training" is another name for sensitivity training, it seems likely that Fitch was familiar with NTL and its methods.

DIM worried about "imposing its own ethno-centric standards on a black man and without intending it, set[ting] up false expectations of [Fitch]" before his arrival. To help, staff underwent a series of group sessions with black NTL trainer Orian Worden.[12] Notably, Fitch was required to meet a lower professional standard than the rest of the staff. Campbell would regularly press white staff

---

9. Terry, "Action from the Boundary," 383.
10. Black Congress of Los Angeles details from Bloom and Martin, *Black Against Empire*, 140-143.
    Angela Davis details from Biography.com Editors, "Angela Davis Biography."
11. Terry, "Action from the Boundary," 383.
12. Terry, "Action from the Boundary," 386.
    Worden was senior enough at NTL that he would be a part of the committee to help select Bradford's replacement after Bennis backed out of the job. Bradford, *National Training Laboratories*, 196.

to turn in paperwork while not doing the same to Fitch.[13] DIM's efforts made little difference. Despite their close relationship—Fitch and his wife lived with Terry and his wife upon the Fitch's move to Detroit—Fitch quit after 19 months. Terry recalled Fitch's time on staff as "agonizing, marked by occasional open confrontation but more frequently characterized by suppressed frustration and increasing suspicion and mistrust."[14]

Fitch's loyalty to DIM, or lack thereof, was a cause of much of the conflict. The rest of the staff considered their first professional loyalty to be to their employer, but Fitch considered his first professional loyalty to be to the black community. Shortly after beginning work, he found himself specifically directing his loyalty to the League of Revolutionary Black Workers, a militant and explicitly Marxist-Leninist labor organization for black workers who felt the United Auto Workers was insufficiently radical to represent them.[15] The League also took inspiration from Mao Zedong and was absorbed into the Communist League in 1971.[16]

As a primarily communist organization, the League was only interested in organizing for the minority of black workers who had allied themselves with the communist cause.[17] Fitch, via DIM, worked closely with the League and its founding chapter the Dodge Revolutionary Union Movement, which had been described by UAW members as "anarchist, violent toward persons, and basically didn't want to solve the problems they were raising."[18] As an example of their violence, League member Rushie Forge stabbed his

---

13. Terry, "Action from the Boundary," 398.
14. Terry, "Action from the Boundary," 388.
15. Terry, "Action from the Boundary," 388–389.
    League description from Ahmad, "League of Revolutionary Black Workers."
16. Maoist inspiration from Kelly and Betsy, *Black like Mao*.
    Absorption into the Communist League from Georgakas and Surkin, *Detroit*.
17. Geschwender, *Class, Race, and Worker Insurgency*, 150.
18. Terry, "Action from the Boundary," 370.

foreman, and the League praised him for it as a hero resisting the oppressive white capitalist system.[19] League members would regularly refer to their white coworkers as "racist pig," "honkey," "pollack," and "devil," even when there was no evidence of racial prejudice from those white colleagues.[20] Following in line with the League's radical strategies, and very different from other DIM staff, Fitch would tell industrial managers, "I know you wouldn't do anything if you weren't scared and we weren't breathing down your neck. And that's good."[21]

Fitch developed and presented his racial philosophy in an article entitled, "Doing My Thing," which was published by DIM. In the article, Fitch distinguished between two broad periods of black development: "African Greatness" and "Exile in Western Hell," with the exile ending in a "New Era" of Black Power. Fitch also expressed his preference for black nationalist Marcus Garvey over more mainstream activists W.E.B. Dubois and Booker T. Washington, whose promotion of assimilation and integration Fitch believed was wrong. Garvey was famous in part for denouncing "miscegenation" and collaborating with the Ku Klux Klan to forward their shared goal of racial separatism.[22] Fitch writes that Stokely Carmichael's development of Black Power was "the most significant of the decisions made by black men down through history," and cites the eponymously-titled book several times, including repeating Charles Silberman's quote that "the United States—all of it, North as well as South, West as well as East—is a racist society [the active and passive operation of

---

19. League of Revolutionary Black Workers, *Spear*.
20. Geschwender, *Class, Race, and Worker Insurgency*, 175.
21. Terry, "Action from the Boundary," 348.
22. Encyclopaedia Britannica. "Marcus Garvey."

anti-black attitudes and practices]" the bracketed definition being added by Fitch and not appearing in Carmichael.[23]

DIM accepted and affirmed Fitch's philosophy. Terry himself had previously written a paper and given lectures promoting Black Power, but Fitch criticized Terry's take on the subject. Fitch told Terry, echoing Carmichael, that "the real issue for the white man was his stance toward himself, not blacks. He needed to work on his own identity in order to discern what he really stood for and what he was really about." With that in mind, Terry went on with Fitch's help to develop a theory of "new white consciousness."[24]

Terry's "new white consciousness" was fully codified in his March 1970 manifesto *For Whites Only*, which sold tens of thousands of copies and raised his profile nationally.[25] The book was dedicated "to Douglass Fitch, a black man who confronted me with my whiteness and challenged me to come to terms with it," and it explicitly cited Carmichael and Hamilton's *Black Power*.[26] As Carmichael advocated, Terry agreed: "Whites often want prematurely to affiliate with blacks on race issues without having begun to attack racism in the white-dominated structures. ... Once whites have begun to act in a concerted and continual effort to combat white racism, then and perhaps only then are they in a position to engage in serious conversation with blacks."[27]

---

23. Fitch, "Life & Work / Doing My Thing."
24. Terry, "Action from the Boundary," 357.
25. Burgin, "The Workshop as the Work," 69.
26. Terry, *For Whites Only*, Dedication.
    Carmichael citation from Terry, *For Whites Only*, 52.
27. Terry, *For Whites Only*, 95.
    Terry's commitment to entirely separate activism was milder than SNCC's. Many of Terry's Racism Awareness Trainings were taught in partnership with Fitch. Terry argued, "some groups fighting racism believe that only whites should deal with whites and only blacks should deal with blacks. It has been my experience that this is an ideological commitment rather than an effective tactic for change. I recognize the ideological point—whites must deal with their own problems rather than treating

That would apparently inform Terry's seductively simple definition of "new white consciousness," which was "an awareness of our whiteness and its role in race problems."[28] The book opens with a quandary: "In response to growing demands, increasing numbers of white Americans fear there is no way to satisfy the black community. Whites seem to be in a no-win situation. Whatever they do is quickly interpreted by some blacks as inadequate, minimal, or racist." So what are whites to do? Stop blaming blacks for their problems and instead realize the condition of blacks is a white problem. Terry quotes the same section of the Kerner Commission report noting that "white society is deeply implicated in the ghetto. White institutions created it, white institutions maintain it, and white society condones it." Quoting Frank Joyce repurposing an old military idiom, Terry explained "'we have met the enemy, and they are *us*.' This insight is part of what we would call *new white consciousness*."[29]

While it is necessary and right to recognize, as the Kerner Commission did, the many ways the white community historically harmed the black community, Terry distorted that uncontroversial fact to support his views. For example, Terry notes that the Kerner Commission stated regarding majority black schools, "equality of results with all-white schools must be the goal." Many might criticize the Kerner Commission on the grounds that equality of opportunity, not equality of results, should be our goal. Terry's criticism, however, was quite different; he wrote, "the report reveals a crippling contradiction. *While white institutions are indicted as the main cause of our racial problems, the same white institutions are used as*

---

blacks as the problem. However, I feel it is false to assume that only whites can do the job. Black and white teams seem to be more effective than whites alone." Terry, *For Whites Only*, 98.

28. Terry, *For Whites Only*, 17.

29. Terry, *For Whites Only*, 11–16.

the standard of success. The solutions were designed to rid America of its black problem by making blacks white."[30]

But there was no question at the time that, on average, black schools were failing their students at a horrifying rate compared to white schools. According to the hugely influential 1966 Coleman Report, which studied differences in schools by racial makeup, the median black 12th-grade student performed 10.9 points worse than their white counterpart on an average of five achievement tests. Looking at math tests specifically, the subject in which accusations of cultural bias are least plausible, black 12th-grade students performed 10 points worse than their white counterparts. [31] The report found that the median black student and white student entered first grade with a difference, but when measuring grade 6, grade 9, and grade 12 students, black students fell further and further behind at each measure. Coleman wrote:

> For most minority groups then, and most particularly the Negro, schools provide little opportunity for them to overcome this initial deficiency; in fact they fall farther behind the white majority in the development of several skills which are critical to making a living and participating fully in modern society. Whatever may be the combination of non-school factors— poverty, community attitudes, low education level of parents—which put minority children at a disadvantage in verbal and nonverbal skills when they enter the first grade, the fact is the schools have not overcome it.[32]

30. Terry, *For Whites Only*, 17.
31. Coleman, *Equality of Educational Opportunity*, 20.
32. Coleman, *Equality of Educational Opportunity*, 21.

In addition to its sobering conclusions about the failure of schools in minority communities, the report's findings also suggest that the educational deficiencies in these communities cannot be attributed to a lack of motivation. Coleman found black students were 1 percent more likely to "do anything to stay in school," 10 percent less likely to be willfully absent, and 25 percent more likely to desire "to be best in class."[33] Coleman found, "it is for the most disadvantaged children that improvements in school quality will make the most difference in achievement."[34]

Yet, in discussing the alleged racism of white liberals, Terry criticized Project Head Start (a Great Society program that aimed to increase the quality of diet and education in failing black schools) by claiming:

The implicit assumption of white liberals is that white dominated and white-controlled institutions and culture are healthy while black counterparts are sick. The liberal, from his self-designated stance of health, is justified then in setting up programs to cure the black from his sickness. Black power exposes this racist myth. Black power calls for white Americans to realize that the deepest sickness lies with the white community, not the black. ... The white liberal is not a source of new humanity, but the perpetuator of white sickness. ... Through liberal "concern for the Negro" the basic problem of pervasive white racism is sidestepped. ... As positive as some of these programs have sounded, they have (unintentionally in many cases) perpetuated an even more serious racist

---

33. Coleman, *Equality of Educational Opportunity*, 24.
34. Coleman, *Equality of Educational Opportunity*, 22.

presupposition. Efforts to overcome alienation by assimilating blacks into the mainstream of American life have presupposed the mainstream as the desirable standard. Equality with whites is the goal. What the liberal does not understand is that equality with whites is a racist goal. ... Integration has been the key word in the liberal's racist vocabulary.[35]

Terry's tactics also aligned with NTL's playbook. NTL considered "discussion about other groups," specifically discussion of problems arising in other groups, to be an obstacle to inspiring the necessary changes within a group. Groups must instead focus on their own need for change.[36] Terry further explains:

Most discussions of racism identify two places for its expression—institutions and individuals. This distinction is extremely important because it makes clear that well-intentioned people can perpetuate racism in institutions even though they themselves have never personally engaged in overt acts of racial injustice. As valuable as this distinction is, it ignores another crucial place for analysis—the cultural or belief system of the American that sets his orientation in the decision-making process.[37]

As an example of this, Terry asks his reader to consider how racism is allegedly encoded into our everyday language: "some words have emotional content that is not always easy to specify. Two

35. Terry, *For Whites Only*, 53–55.
36. Bradford, *National Training Laboratories*, Appendix 212.
37. Terry, *For Whites Only*, 43.

such words are white and black. Whiteness is celebrated as a good while blackness is castigated as bad. To test this observation, try to think of derogatory uses of white. White lie? No, a white lie is an acceptable lie. In the same regard, try to think of good uses of black."[38] Complicating the point that Terry intends to make with this example is the fact that similar black-white symbolism also exists in historic African cultures. For example, white signifies purity and beauty to the Igbo people of southeastern Nigeria. Black represents "antisocial behaviors that should be avoided" to Nigeria's Ibibo people. In most human cultures, blackness has been symbolically associated with the nighttime and the fear the dark can bring, while white light is positively associated with the daytime.[39] Or consider that by just a slight shift in language choice, one finds the word "pale" usually has a negative valence, while "colorful" has a positive valence. But weak examples like this would be enough for Terry to argue, "the attack on institutional and individual racism fails to show the extent of a racist mentality that legitimates and justifies institutional and individual acts of racism," where "racist mentality" means simply not agreeing with Terry's worldview that all of America is culturally racist.

On those grounds, Terry argued that "none of us escapes being racist in American society. All of us participate in racist thought forms as well as institutional practices."[40] Rephrased, this meant to Terry and his intellectual followers that all white people are racist by definition; the best a white person can be is an "anti-racist racist."[41]

---

38. Terry, *For Whites Only*, 45.
39. McNatt, "Unmasking the Meaning Behind Color in African Art."
40. Terry, *For Whites Only*, 66.
41. While Terry does not use the term "anti-racist racist" in the cited materials, his contemporaries explained his position as such. Katz, "A Systematic Handbook of Exercises for the Re-Education of White People with Respect to Racist Attitudes and Behaviors," 295.

Arriving at and accepting this "consciousness," Terry believed, was necessary for white people to be able to fight for positive change, writing, "the only way for whites to get into the conversation is for them to admit that they are racists, and to commit themselves to attack racism and begin the arduous task of working to eliminate it."[42]

Although Terry relied heavily on the term "cultural racism" in *For Whites Only*, a few years later, in 1972, Harvard social psychologist James M. Jones claimed in his book *Prejudice & Racism* to have coined it himself. Like Terry, Jones' use of the term cultural racism is derived from his assumption that it is a form of racism to consider some cultural traits superior to others when those cultural traits align with race.[43] As an example of cultural racism, Jones alleges that African culture utilizes "magic and superstition," while Western culture utilizes "rational thought." On these grounds, Jones criticizes considering "White Western-European ... science, and medicine" inherently superior as a form of cultural racism.[44]

To many, it would seem uncontroversial to value "rational thought," including its byproducts "science" and "medicine," over "magic and superstition." The countless Africans whose lives have been improved tremendously by innovations in science and medicine would likely be the first to speak to that truth. This isn't to say that genuine cultural racism doesn't exist. For example, white Americans often look down on black Americans for speaking in black vernacular English instead of speaking how the majority of whites speak, or for different cultural styles of dress not fitting in with white upper-class culture. There is no reason that speaking English in a different dialect or dressing differently ought to inform

---

42. Terry, *For Whites Only*, 96.
43. Terry used "cultural racism" first in Terry, *For Whites Only*, 66.
44. Jones, *Prejudice and Racism*, 6.

white Americans' views of black Americans' intelligence or ability to be successful in the world. Insofar as white Americans discriminate against such cultural traits, it's entirely appropriate to inform white Americans that such discrimination is unethical and to work to put a stop to it.

But when "cultural racism" is taken to mean valuing *any* cultural traits more than others, it becomes philosophically incoherent. This position is known as "cultural relativism," and it has been widely discredited in the field of philosophy. The position is self-defeating; cultures do not survive unless the people within them believe their culture is superior to other existing cultures and thus should be maintained and defended. Cultural relativism is itself a cultural view that views itself as correct and superior to competing cultural views.[45] Taken to its logical conclusion, it would imply that acts such as female genital mutilation, honor killings, and infanticide—all of which are commonly practiced in large societies even today—cannot be described as objectively wrong, or that cultures that prohibit such acts are objectively better.[46]

As it applies to Terry, is using "white institutions" as the "standard of success" wrong? Perhaps it is, in certain situations. But to totalize this idea, wherein it becomes unacceptable to use any so-called "white" standards of success to criticize the performance of black schools, would entail abandoning underprivileged black children to languish in failing schools. This same logic applies to other problems such as crime, fatherlessness, and poor diet that disproportionately harm the black community and are at least

---

45. Jones did understand this criticism, writing "it is unreasonable to think there are no values or adaptations that are universally good-necessary to adaptive human survival." However, he did not provide any meaningful counterargument, simply stating that despite this "the hegemony enjoyed by the absolute view suggests the relative view merits favor." Jones, *Prejudice and Racism*, 159.
46. Rachels, "The Challenge of Cultural Relativism."

partially attributable to culture. Under Terry's philosophy, we are asked not only to pretend these are not problems at all, but also to consider any suggestion that they are problems a form of racism.

But preferring black culture was not a solution for Terry:

> Some whites, having recognized the futility of being indifferent to color, have taken another tack. They have identified with blacks so completely that they want to deny their own whiteness. They talk like blacks, dress like blacks, read mostly black literature, listen to black music, pick up most clues about what to think from blacks ... New whiteness challenges whites who attempt to live off black consciousness and black power. New whiteness questions the radical hate many of these whites have for whiteness.

Terry, like anti-integrationists Fitch and Carmichael, wanted people to identify more with their race rather than less.

> The idea of new white consciousness has puzzled many people. A first impression for some is that it is a step backward rather than forward. The emphasis on color, they argue, only serves to perpetuate division. Instead of being color-conscious, we should be color-blind. ... Protestations to deny whiteness eliminate neither the fact nor the problem of white privilege. ... To dissociate oneself from whiteness by affirming humanness ignores what whiteness has done and how we continue to benefit from it.[47]

---

47. Terry, *For Whites Only*, 17–20.

Asking white people to identify more with their whiteness, of course, runs the risk of backfiring. While Terry's intent was clearly to use new white consciousness to aid Black Power and black self-determination, it's difficult to predict how the idea would actually function in society once let loose (assuming, reasonably, that not all white people would agree with the totality of Terry's philosophy). Historically, close identification with one's race, including both whites in the West and other racial majority groups worldwide, has been a necessary ingredient leading to horrific, violent racism. Colorblind anti-racism aimed to solve this by decreasing the salience of all racial identities. But if we take the position that in order to oppose racism, we must oppose Western culture for being "white" and considering itself superior to other cultures, as Terry did, colorblindness can't be allowed. The entire culture whites are raised in becomes racist by definition.

Terry proposes a new definition of racism: *"any activity by individuals, groups, institutions, or cultures that treats human beings unjustly because of color and rationalizes that treatment by attributing to them undesirable biological, psychological, social, or cultural characteristics."*[48] The numerous possible ways of defining "unjustly" notwithstanding, the first half of Terry's definition is uncontroversial. Treating human beings unjustly because of their skin color is akin to the traditional dictionary definition of racism. But the second half of this definition, that such treatment is rationalized by attributing it to undesirable characteristics, prevents any legitimate inquiry into causes and cures for group differences. "Undesirable biological" characteristics echoes the racist pseudoscience of old, but what about "social" and "cultural" characteristics?

Terry explains that he included this language "because most

---

48. Terry, *For Whites Only*, 41.

whites deny that color is the reason for rejecting blacks," denying any possibility that claim might be true in most or even any cases. Terry quotes Frank Joyce with some examples of such alleged rationalizations, "police are given excessive power in the ghetto not to deny basic constitutional rights to second-class-citizen black people but stop 'crime in the streets.' Blacks are not denied jobs because of their skin color but because they are not 'qualified.'"[49] But these don't appear to be rationalizations, at least not in most instances. When education is so much worse in the black community, an outcome will be that there is a smaller pool of qualified black candidates for higher-skill jobs. If we want to fix that problem, calling any social reasoning a "rationalization" rather than recognizing it as a fact will provide the wrong solution. There is a large literature on "mismatch," the phenomenon of individuals being placed in schools or jobs that they would not have gotten into without the help of affirmative action, failing in those positions, as where they could have succeeded in the placements they would have received without affirmative action.[50] Asking companies to hire unqualified candidates will create bad outcomes for both those companies and the employees seen as failing on the job, but creating more qualified black candidates will create good outcomes both for the company and the employee.

With institutional and cultural racism so baked into the American system, what anti-racist solutions did Terry consider effective? Sometimes extreme policy changes such as reappraising and changing our "understanding of private property—whether it be a car or stock in General Motors," engaging in "serious study of other economic systems," including those of then-communist Yugoslavia

---

49. Terry, *For Whites Only*, 41.
50. For more see Sander and Taylor, *Mismatch*.

and Cuba, and also, possibly, revolutionary violence.[51] Terry considered "unjust social system" a form of "'systematic,' 'structural,' or 'figurative' violence."[52] Given this, Terry felt that retaliatory revolutionary violence could be justified, though he wasn't enthusiastic about it, noting that "violence can be suicidal as well as productive," but that "attacks on property and persons ... may be necessary. If all other avenues for change fail to dislodge racism."[53] It is important also to remember that, for Terry, to "dislodge racism" means to overthrow all of white America's culture, not ending racial prejudice.

But Terry and the Detroit Industrial Mission knew they didn't have the ability to end racism in all of society by themselves. So how did Terry believe racism could be cured in organizations? "A training program on new whiteness."[54] Although DIM had secularized much of their work, it was still grounded in a religious mode of thinking; Terry wrote of a prior curriculum of DIM's, "a theological note: One of the problems in our curriculum is that we expect salvation before repentance."[55] After completing his new social justice framework, he would refer to it as "a religion of the republic."[56]

---

51. Terry, *For Whites Only*, 76–77 and 80.
52. Terry, *For Whites Only*, 79.
    This view was not original to Terry. He cites it to Hough, "The Christian, Violence, and Social Change."
    Hough was a friend of Fitch's and would later work with Terry. Hough, "Letter to Robert Terry on the July 23, 1969."
53. Terry, *For Whites Only*, 85 and 91.
54. Terry, *For Whites Only*, 74.
55. Terry, "Action from the Boundary," 337.
56. Terry, "Action from the Boundary," 380.

The Detroit Industrial Mission Spreads "New White Consciousness"

DIM intended to develop a curriculum package on racism as early as the spring of 1968. The same month Fitch was hired, the staff agreed, after being pushed by Terry, to move forward on the program. Terry had already been asked to lead a multi-week discussion at Royal Oak Baptist Church on "White Racism and Black Power," which would inform his work designing DIM's curriculum. People Against Racism's material would also inform DIM's curriculum from its inception.[1]

In the summer and fall of 1968, a pilot curriculum was tested at two churches, the Jefferson Avenue Baptist Church and the Presbyterian Church of Our Savior. Terry considered both of these tests "frustrating and unsatisfying." Terry was not the lead designer of the curriculum's first iteration, and he believed the problem with this early version was that it "suggested subtly that blacks needed whites to help blacks become part of the American mainstream."

---

1. Terry, *For Whites Only*, 358.

This disagreement drove Terry to create brand new materials and teaching methods based around new white consciousness.[2]

DIM needed a testing ground for Terry's new ideas. Conveniently, in August of 1968, the New Detroit Committee established a volunteer Speaker's Bureau with Robert Terry's wife Jo-Ann Terry as its leader. Fitch and Robert Terry were both directly involved in the bureau's operations.[3] Participation in Terry's new white consciousness seminars usually appeared to be self-selecting, with those inclined to agree with him choosing to attend. That certainly was the case at a "volunteer" Speaker's Bureau, as Terry found that in many of the seminars, after Terry would open with the question "what does it mean to be white today," participants would often include negative words such as "angry," "frustrated," "inadequate," "insecure," and "guilty."[4]

Terry preached that "dialogue as a tactic should be a regular tool of the new white, to be used with neighbors, friends, and any institutional setting." However, the radical views of new white consciousness often weren't taken well. New Detroit's speakers regularly faced personal consequences for attempting to evangelize new white consciousness: "A number of New Detroit speakers have found that their suburban friends no longer invite them to social gatherings or to their homes. A number of them have felt isolation and loneliness because they have been ostracized by their own community." Terry believed that an antidote to this would be to organize "new whites" into their own social groups, in essence desiring to create an ideological cult.[5]

Dialogue was not Terry's only teaching mechanism. He considered confrontation a stronger tactic:

---

2. Terry, *For Whites Only*, 359.
3. Terry, "Action from the Boundary," 360.
4. Terry, *New Whites*, 5.
5. Terry, *For Whites Only*, 87.

An example of this approach was a session recently conducted by the New Detroit Speakers Bureau to train new speakers. A number of black and white consultants trained in group work, as well as black and white consciousness, designed a training session that included confrontation. Three content areas were programmed into the two-day event—black consciousness, white institutional racism, and new white consciousness. Following each major presentation a two-and-a-half-hour small group session was held. The plan called for the major learning experiences to occur in the small groups. In order to facilitate that process, a black and white team was assigned to lead each group, one of the leaders being particularly skilled in one of the content areas and the other skilled in group process.

About a day and a half into the conference, the blacks called a caucus. All the blacks left to go to another room while the whites sat alone in the lecture hall—stunned and bewildered. Some whites were suspicious that the caucus had been planned by the leadership. Others were upset that blacks and whites were separated. In reality, the caucus was not premeditated but grew out of the dynamics of the meeting. But it forced the whites to come to terms with themselves in a way that they never had done before.

The agenda for the rest of the day was cancelled and the whites had to create their own agenda for the remainder of the afternoon. One group of whites was so shattered by the day-and-a-half experience that they formed themselves into the "125 Percent

Shattered Group" to try to make some sense out of what was happening. Other whites formed into small intense discussion groups dealing with institutional racism and new white consciousness. One group formed a discussion to figure out procedures by which to deal with the possible demands from the black caucus.

Two hours after the black caucus convened, they returned to place their demands before the total meeting. They did not ask for white support. Rather they said they would work in the speakers bureau, but they also demanded a hearing before the Board of Directors of the New Detroit Committee to confront that board with the racism within the organization itself.

The whites were forced into a dilemma. What should they do with the demand of the black caucus? Should they simply let it be read? Should they support it? Should they write their own amendment to it? After much hassling and public debate, the white caucus finally supported the demand, promising to work to guarantee the hearing before the Board of Directors and also independently or together with the black caucus to work to eliminate racism at New Detroit, Incorporated.

This confrontation between black and white was agonizing for many whites. Most had never been in this kind of situation. Many had never met or talked with articulate, middle-class, angry blacks. The overall result of this kind of confrontation was extremely valuable and useful. Of the eighty-four whites in attendance, at least 80 percent responded positively to this confrontation and deepened their own insight, understanding, and commitment to fight racism as a result of it. Some whites were extremely threatened by the event and reacted with great hostility. In balance, the designers of the conference felt that the confrontation tactic was a valuable tool for change, especially change of consciousness.[6]

This conflict-oriented style is a hallmark of NTL's T-Group methods. It is also shockingly similar to NTL's own internal conflict with a Black Caucus. Terry noted that this "confrontation design" could be modified into "a straight sensitivity group approach."[7] Although Terry found confrontation a valuable tactic, he felt that it must be "accompanied by new white analysis." Since confrontation heightened "white guilt, defensiveness, and anger," whites must be provided with a way "to make sense out of the black rage or their own responses."[8] As NTL had discovered through their work, "group members find that their basic anxiety problems tend to disappear at the point of their accurate diagnosis and acceptance."[9] Of course what appears "accurate" is not necessarily so, but so long as group members feel that they can do something, that diagnosis and acceptance provides a psychological reward of anxiety reduction.

With the experience at the Speakers' Bureau under their belt, Fitch and Terry were able to pitch Michigan Bell Telephone on teaching their curriculum to staff. Bell already had an anti-racist training program in place that focused on teaching staff about the problems in the ghetto and examining the causes of poverty, but

---

6. Terry, *For Whites Only*, 87–88.
7. Terry, *For Whites Only*, 88.
8. Terry, *For Whites Only*, 89–90.
9. Bradford, *National Training Laboratories*, Appendix 298.

Fitch raised questions on that focus: "How were whites going to train whites to deal with blacks? And, second, was not the racial focus misplaced? Blacks weren't the problem, whites were. Why not examine white racism in the company?"[10] Bell hired Fitch and Terry to make those changes.

Fitch and Terry taught new white consciousness to Bell's on-staff trainers using an early manuscript of *For Whites Only*. However, it wasn't immediately integrated into Bell's programs. Fitch engaged in Bell's business more frequently than Terry, and Fitch with a leader of the League of Revolutionary Black Workers led an anti-racism training for top Bell management. However, the participants in Fitch's training got so angry and frustrated with the event that Fitch brought in Terry to try to pivot the training and ease tensions. This gave Terry the opportunity to teach new white consciousness directly to Bell's management. Terry recalled that "sharp exchanges between whites and blacks ensued, one man almost leaving the room." But nonetheless, enough of the participants came away feeling that "all Bell management should experience this kind of confrontation and reconstruction." Bell integrated new white consciousness into the core of its training program.[11]

The experience at Bell led Fitch and Terry to the opportunity in 1969 to teach at AT&T.[12] Around that same time, the General Motors Institute (GMI) also hired Fitch and Terry to teach.[13] Although they faced some opposition at GMI, teaching at GMI

---

10. Terry, "Action from the Boundary," 360.
11. Terry, "Action from the Boundary," 361–362.
12. Terry, "Action from the Boundary," 363.
13. At the time, the General Motors Institute was a trade school fully owned by General Motors and designed to teach people to work in the automotive industry. The school still exists, but in 1982 it split off from General Motors and in 1998 it was renamed Kettering University. Kettering University. "1919 to 2019."

would prove to be a major opportunity to spread their ideas; GMI videotaped Fitch and Terry's presentations to show at a meeting of the National Association of Businessmen in Washington, and to continue using at the school in Fitch and Terry's physical absence.[14] A middle manager at General Electric who was a volunteer for the Speaker's Bureau helped Terry pitch his program to General Electric leadership, which eventually led to a cross-corporate training featuring representatives from General Electric, General Motors, Ford, Chrysler, and Whitehead & Kales.[15] Terry would also continue to teach at churches, conducting an eight-week seminar at Birmingham Presbyterian Church.[16] Although the vast majority of their work took place in Michigan, Terry and Fitch traveled as far as the School of Theology at Claremont, California to teach a two-day seminar to staff on new white consciousness.[17] And Terry would work with the National Industrial Mission to coordinate with other chapters.[18]

Perhaps Fitch, Terry, and DIM's biggest break was when they were prominently featured in a March 1969, PBS film *Do You Think a Job Is the Answer?* The film argued that jobs for black Americans were not a sufficient solution for their community, but instead, white Americans needed to look deeper at their racist roots.[19] Even after Fitch's departure from DIM, his ideas continued to spread, with NTL's Orian Worden taking Fitch's place to teach with Terry at automotive company Borg & Beck. By that point, New White Consciousness seminars had become "the crux of the training

14. Terry, "Action from the Boundary," 364–365.
15. Terry, "Action from the Boundary," 367.
16. Terry, "Action from the Boundary," 374.
17. Hough, "Letter to Robert Terry on October 15, 1969."
18. Terry, "Action from the Boundary," 410.
19. Terry, "Action from the Boundary," 366 and PBS, 1968.

events that the Mission staged for corporations."[20] Their trainings at Borg and Beck included screening the film *Black Power*, which featured Stokely Carmichael giving a speech to the Black Panthers, and they succeeded in convincing the company to end its non-discrimination policy.[21]

Fitch & Terry appear together in Do You Think a Job Is the Answer?

Despite Fitch and Terry's apparent success in spreading their philosophy, all was not well inside DIM staff meetings. At the height of their new white and black consciousness work, the meetings were "emotion laden" and "confrontational." In addition to Fitch's loyalty problems, Doug White (who also appeared in the PBS film with

20. Burgin, "The Workshop as the Work," 87–89.

In 1978, Orian Worden would become one of three members of a "Task Force on the Reorganization of NTL," bringing into NTL's mission the principle that the distribution of identity categories including "race" "should be a continuing, important criteria for the evolvement [sic] of the organization." Hirsch, "A History of the NTL Institute for Applied Behavioral Science," 107–108.

21. Burgin, "The Workshop as the Work," 96 and 105.

Fitch and Terry), felt that "Terry was using new white consciousness as a stick to beat down the staff."[22] Conversely, Terry felt that the rest of the staff had not struggled enough with his concept of new white consciousness, and Fitch felt that except for Terry, the rest of the staff "was not deeply committed to combating racism." When DIM considered hiring another black man, Fitch challenged them. "'Why hire a black?' he asked. 'To do what?' 'The same thing as whites?'"[23] Fitch and Terry were also engaged in a financial dispute with DIM, as they had accepted personal fees for services rendered at New Detroit, Bell, and elsewhere on DIM staff time. When DIM decided to ban accepting money personally for DIM-type activities, Fitch and Terry were so infuriated that they considered purposefully violating the rule in protest.[24] DIM's funding was an issue too. DIM had not communicated effectively with its denominational funders about their anti-racism work, and this contributed to a decline in church funding. However, DIM was able to make up for this loss by charging fees for their services and procuring large-scale industry funding in the form of grants from Chrysler and Ford.[25]

Another disagreement among staff members was on how radical their methodology should be. DIM needed continued access to and support from their industry partners, and some staff members feared that these partners might end their relationship with DIM if they felt DIM's agenda was too radical. But many also worried that, if they weren't radical enough, DIM might be assimilated into the existing industrial culture. For example, "D.I.M. understood the necessity for strategic violence in certain situations to counteract systemic violence perpetuated by an unjust social and positical [sic]

---

22. Terry, "Action from the Boundary," 390–391.
23. Terry, "Action from the Boundary," 396.
24. Terry, "Action from the Boundary," 391–394.
25. Terry, "Action from the Boundary," 414–417.

system. But as an organization it could not publicly support it."[26] The staff agreed that their vision of justice was similar to "radical groups," having come to accept "the angering reality that injustice in America penetrated to the heart of the country," that "power" needed to be "a major variable in any social theory D.I.M. would entertain seriously," and that "Marxism" needed to become "a serious resource for D.I.M." However, given their professional relationships, they needed to use different methods than other radical groups.[27] DIM solved this by adopting what they called an "insider/outsider" strategy.[28]

The staff believed America was in a "pre-revolutionary" period, but that a successful mass uprising wouldn't be possible without substantial work "radicalizing people inside and outside the large corporations in America." DIM, having secured access to industrial organizations, recognized that they "could educate, radicalize and persuade inside power figures," but they also "needed outside pressure to escalate inside action and thereby force management and labor to deal with the issues." Corporations "needed inside consultants with a radical analysis to influence the way corporate decision makers responded to external pressure." Meanwhile, "outside pressure increased D.I.M.'s power by creating a need for D.I.M.'s service."[29]

With the 21st-century proliferation of corporate Racism Awareness Training in the tradition of Terry, it appears this strategy is being practiced now more than ever before.[30] However, the scale

---

26. Terry, "Action from the Boundary," 424.
27. Terry, "Action from the Boundary," 422, 428, 434, and 443.
28. Terry, "Action from the Boundary," 422.
29. Terry, "Action from the Boundary," 422–423.
30. Proof of takeoff of corporate trainings from Judkis, "Anti-Racism Trainers Were Ready for This Moment."

of the strategy's success remains in question.[31] Less in question is the effectiveness of spreading Terry's ideology in the educational sector, performed not as much by Terry himself as those he influenced.

---

31. Dobbin and Kalev, "Why Doesn't Diversity Training Work?"

The Effort to Redefine Racism
Enters Education

In 1969, the United States National Student Association (USNSA), which just two years prior had been involved in a major scandal after Ramparts magazine revealed that a large portion of their operations had been funded and controlled by the CIA, published an anthology of essays titled *Racism and Higher Education.*[1] Among an essay claiming that the idea of an American melting-pot "helped to create and maintain racism," a Marxist essay written by the "National Secretary of the Independent Socialist Clubs," an essay arguing "White America should stop activities where they interact with residents of the Black poverty community in a helping role," and others was a piece titled, "Racism In America —Definition And Analysis" by David Steinberg, based on materials from People Against Racism—the group founded by Frank Joyce that claimed "conscious motivation" was irrelevant to calling something racist.[2] Citing extensively from Stokely Carmichael,

---

1. Agee, "The National Student Association Scandal."
2. Melting-pot quote from Isgar and Isgar, *Racism and Higher Education*, 4.

Steinberg sought to draw a distinction "between prejudice and bigotry on the one hand, and racism on the other." Perhaps even more radical than Bidol's "Power + Prejudice" redefinition, Steinberg argued that "prejudice, the belief that whites are superior to people of color, is altogether different from racism," defining racism as "the political, social, economic, status, and psychological systems [white people] created to make their stereotypes come true."[3] Steinberg explained that "the real problem of racism in America does not lie with individuals, but with the 'system,' the ways in which individual behavior are socially structured." Working from People Against Racism's material, Steinberg echoed Joyce's concept of "behavioral racism," individual racism in which it is not necessary to find any conscious racist motive so long as the actions lead to unequal outcomes.[4] Steinberg argued that even without any "malicious intent" from whites, racism would continue for as long as "the housing market" was allowed to "function freely," "landlords" were allowed to "pursue their right to maximize profit," and "employers ... hire those most competent for the job."[5] Like Carmichael and Terry, Steinberg's solution to racism meant overthrowing the entire system, which he defined as "the American way."[6]

Informed by Steinberg, the full "racism staff" of the USNSA

Steinberg's essay would also be distributed by People Acting for Change Together, a successor group to the New Detroit Speakers' Bureau and still chaired by Jo Ann Terry, which will be discussed in depth in Part 2. Katz, *White Awareness*, 204.

Ironically, the Marxist essay in *Racism & Higher Education* written by Sy Landy would argue that "it is a middle class liberal myth to believe that anti-racism education can solve the problem of racism." Isgar and Isgar, *Racism and Higher Education*, 31.

3. Isgar and Isgar, *Racism and Higher Education*, 14.
4. Isgar and Isgar, *Racism and Higher Education*, 15.
5. Isgar and Isgar, *Racism and Higher Education*, 16.
6. Isgar and Isgar, *Racism and Higher Education*, 14.

agreed that "racism is the 'American way'" and would come to a very similar definition:

 Racism is the collection of white actions which, *regardless of their intent*, disadvantage people of color to the advantage of white people. Racism and prejudice are mutually supportive, but not the same. Prejudice is the belief that non-white people are inferior to white people; racism is the structuring of societal institutions and mores in such a way as to make the belief in white superiority supportable by "observable" fact.

Racism is the social, political, and economic means by which our institutions can function to guarantee that white privilege remains a social reality.[7]

On the grounds of that definition, the USNSA regarded the "early 60's civil rights groups" and more recent groups with similar ideas as "not truly committed to the end of racism and white privilege."[8] For the USNSA, even legislation was insufficient structural change because the entire system needed to be overturned: "it is impossible to write a law against more black babies dying proportional to white babies or to write a law against the continuing gap in white and nonwhite income, housing and health levels."[9] Like Terry, they agreed that "because there are no parallel institutions or counter-institutions in this society in which people who define themselves as individual anti-racists can participate, all

---

7. Isgar and Isgar, *Racism and Higher Education*, 47.
8. Isgar and Isgar, *Racism and Higher Education*, 47.
9. Isgar and Isgar, *Racism and Higher Education*, 47–48.

of us are institutionally racist. We may choose to become anti-racist in our individual actions. We cannot choose to disengage ourselves totally from the institutions of the society and so act in institutionally non-racist ways."[10] The steps the USNSA wanted to take toward changing that included reforming education so that white people would "study and learn to act on the white problem in America."[11] They considered sensitivity training a "crucial" and "integral" tool for learning human relations skills and to communicate their views more effectively.[12]

Another Detroit-based organization aligned with New Detroit, Inc. and the Detroit Industrial Mission also took up the fight: the Michigan-Ohio Regional Educational Laboratory (MOREL), "a private non-profit corporation supported in part as a regional educational laboratory by funds from the United States Office of Education, Department of Health, Education and Welfare."[13] After the Kerner Commission Report was published, MOREL decided that the theme of "combating racism and its effects" should guide its new curriculum planning efforts. Additionally, MOREL had decided that their operations should be designed to promote "self-renewal," by which they meant "increasingly skillful use of self-analysis, self-definition of goals, and self-directed efforts to change behaviors."[14] At the time, former Deputy Superintendent of the Wayne County Board of Education Delmo Della-Dora (a white man) was MOREL's Director of Planning and Development. He was in charge of the creation of such new programs.[15]

---

10. Isgar and Isgar, *Racism and Higher Education*, 49.

11. Isgar and Isgar, *Racism and Higher Education*, 51.

12. Isgar and Isgar, *Racism and Higher Education*, 64.

13. Della-Dora, *Planning New Development Efforts Recommended Procedures*.

14. Della-Dora, *Planning New Development Efforts Recommended Procedures*, 1.

15. Della-Dora, *Planning New Development Efforts Recommended Procedures*.
    Della-Dora, "The Culturally Disadvantaged," 467.

In May 1969, MOREL published *Racism & Education: A Review of Selected Literature Related to Segregation, Discrimination, and Other Aspects of Racism in Education*. The review was "conducted under the direction of Dr. Delmo Della-Dora" by his staff and was made up near-exclusively of excerpts from and summaries of education scholars' work, in part to gather information to help guide MOREL's future development efforts.[16] The book featured no mention of New Detroit, DIM, Terry, or Carmichael. While it certainly contained material that could be criticized, the closest thing to an extreme citation in the book was relegated to the appendices, where People Against Racism, Frank Joyce, and SNCC were included as bullet points in a much longer list of "experts" and "organizations and/or [a]ssociations ... which would be 'most helpful' to contact for services and/or guidance in the area of field work being done in race relations."[17] The excerpts instead cited more mainstream sources.[18]

One source excerpted and summarized was the "findings and recommendations" from the "co-chairman for the Detroit Board of Education of a High School Study Commission in 1967–68." Those recommendations were overwhelmingly positive, including that "every effort should be made to strengthen education offerings in the schools in a manner that more fully meets the needs of Negro students and to reverse conditions which generally accompany 'racial isolation'"; "the course in American history required of all students at the high school level must include Negro history"; and "base promotional opportunity on merit and make it available to all qualified employees on a city-wide basis." But with the intent of promoting those goals, it included a more far-reaching

---

16. Della-Dora, *Racism and Education,* iii.
17. Della-Dora, *Racism and Education,* 87, 90, 91, and 92.
18. Della-Dora, *Racism and Education,* 9.

recommendation that "a massive in-service education program should be undertaken for the teaching staff in all high schools."[19]

Another cited education report suggested "emphasis should be placed on the education and re-education of administrators, supervisors, and long-term professionals who are in control of school system [sic]. ... In the judgment of the writers we are long overdue for a critical re-education of the professional staff of school systems."[20] Della-Dora and MOREL appeared to discard most of the liberal views contained in the material they collected while retaining more radical strategies.

MOREL complained in their review of the literature that "there really are no programs or research activities that deal directly with institutional racism in the United States." This is unsurprising since the term "institutional racism" was first published in *Black Power* only two years earlier. The suggestions offered throughout the literature largely focused on helping black students and fighting discrimination, such as that teachers should learn how to help "urban disadvantaged youth" with learning, social, and emotional adjustment, and that "classes in Negro and Minority history should be required of all students on the undergraduate level."[21] But these sorts of efforts were unsatisfactory for MOREL: "The major emphasis encountered by the writers in the search for information was that of the 'disadvantaged.' Again, no major effort seems to be in existence which has as its primary aim attempting to prevent, alleviate, or change racist attitudes."[22] To address this "need," MOREL had to create something brand new.

Racism & Education revealed that MOREL was familiar with sensitivity training and NTL. It included a summary of an NEA

19. Della-Dora, *Racism and Education*, 14–15.
20. Della-Dora, *Racism and Education*, 65.
21. Della-Dora, *Racism and Education*, 57–58.
22. Della-Dora, *Racism and Education*, 57.

report promoting NTL and arguing "the importance of sensitivity training" and "that human relations must become a pervasive influence at all levels of the educational operation, involving everyone, vertically from the superintendent to the ghetto janitor, and horizontally from the voice of the ghetto to the private inner sanctums of the jet set." It stated that "local and state associations should assume the leadership role in instituting this training. It is incumbent on local groups to become the agents of change."[23]

MOREL decided to work towards its goal of self-renewal by conducting a "self-examination concerning racism as it manifests itself within the society and within the MOREL staff." In doing so, Della-Dora came to very Carmichael-esque conclusions, writing that "an understanding of what the problems are cannot emerge adequately in combating racism, for example, by going to the very best literature available, nor to the so-called experts. The nature of racism is such that only a few white people understand what being white is in a racist society and, at present, only a minority of Negroes perceive 'the black experience' in our society through black eyes."[24]

Della-Dora recounts that MOREL's self-examination of racism's causes and effects "produced a wide variance of anxiety levels among staff members ranging from mild to unbearable." Nonetheless, "members of the Planning and Development Division [were] unanimous in their feeling that such activities [were] necessary and fruitful for planning and development." Among the rest of the staff, the reception was more mixed, with up to six staff members feeling "that time for staff self-confrontation on racism should be reduced or eliminated."[25]

It's not surprising that this exercise would lead to anxiety. Per

23. Della-Dora, *Racism and Education*, 12.
24. Della-Dora, *Planning New Development Efforts Recommended Procedures*, 11.
25. Della-Dora, *Planning New Development Efforts Recommended Procedures*, 12.

Carmichael's definition of institutional racism, if a society without full equality of representation is racist, and all of white America is complicit in maintaining the status quo for not working to tear down all of its institutions, then accepting this view as truth would naturally lead to immense feelings of guilt over not having done more. Indeed, this sense of anxiety would become common among whites who accepted black radical views. Della-Dora explained what he felt must be done, along with his own redefinition of racism building on Carmichael's "institutional racism":

 The fact of the matter is that there is no basic research which really deals in a meaningful fashion with racism or any of its major components. What is described by this term ('racism') is a set of phenomena which operate within a social-cultural matrix in which individuals either actively contribute to or actively work against racist behaviors and practices.[26] There really is no middle ground for action, any more than there was for Germans who lived in Nazi Germany while 6,000,000 Jews were being murdered. To participate, without protest, in processes and institutions of a society dominated by white people which systematically discriminates against black people in all aspects of living is to be a racist in deed if not by conscious intent. Those who consciously and deliberately discriminate as individuals add a further measure of impact to the seriousness of the problem. It does not appear likely that white people alone can look past their culturally induced perceptions of this

---

26. Like Frank Joyce's, this redefinition appears to be another direct precursor to Ibram X. Kendi's.

problem and adequately provide for the solution of the problem and the same must be said for black people working alone. 'Racism'—a condition produced by our white society—produces ill effects among white people, many in the pathological sense, which make up the syndrome of racial superiority. <u>This syndrome and its manifestations would continue to exist if every black person were to suddenly vanish from the nation</u>. Black people, are afflicted with the effects of racial inferiority but many have repressed their own black experience just as most white people repress their white experience. Thus, we deal with an issue in which the participants engaged in problem-solving, whether black or white, have already suffered significant distortion of perception and must find ways to go beyond their cultural 'blinders.' Studies of <u>individual</u> prejudices and discriminatory behavior on the part of individuals are of limited value because they do not reflect the measure of dynamic interaction of individual attitudes, knowledge, and behavior with the larger institutional and cultural forces. All of the foregoing could be used to justify only basic research and no development work in the field of racism. However, this writer would argue strongly for basic research, applied research, development work and action projects carried on in a coordinated fashion as the only type of approach likely to result in resolution of the problems.[27]

---

27. Della-Dora, *Planning New Development Efforts Recommended Procedures*, 22–23.

This line of thinking is deeply problematic. For one, like many of the theories previously mentioned, it belittles black people by presuming that they are unable to understand their own experience. It also falsely claims there was no basic research that dealt with racism (recall that earlier Della-Dora rejected using the "so-called experts" and "very best literature available" to understand racism; also recall that the Kerner report itself was many hundreds of pages of research on racism). And its redefinition of racism makes any white person a racist by default—even if they have never taken a single action to support racism—and compares all white people who disagree with Della-Dora's capacious definition of racism to the Germans under Nazi rule who didn't fight back. This comparison is preposterous. The Nazi regime killed approximately 77,000 German citizens for various forms of resistance and sent tens of thousands more to concentration camps, some for simply being suspected of being in the opposition.[28] Surely most people would not claim that German citizens must have been willing to sacrifice their lives to fight against the regime or else they were complicit in the Nazi's atrocities? Not lending any more support to the regime than they were forced to in order to survive ought to be considered protest enough. Those who risked their lives to actively fight the regime, or to shelter Jews, were heroes, but one need not be a hero to not be a racist.

This principle ought to hold even more true in America, where we have democratic processes. Truly racist institutions, such as slavery and Jim Crow, cannot survive without enough people voting to maintain them. By voting against them, one is a part of tearing down institutional racism. But under this new definition of racism, if all of American society is institutionally racist, and one isn't voting to tear down all of American society, then one is complicit.

28. Hoffman, *The History of the German Resistance*, xiii.

Within a few months of beginning MOREL's self-examination exercises on racism, the MOREL Board of Directors decided that not only should combating racism guide new curriculum planning efforts, but "the focus of *all* of MOREL program development should be on ways to undo causes and effects of racism." Staff time and funding were shifted to accommodate this decision.[29] Since at least 1962, Della-Dora believed that it was the role of the schools to initiate action on social problems, which in turn would spur the larger community to coordinate with the schools on solving them.[30]

One of MOREL's pilot programs under this goal was a "Unit on White Racism," designed to teach white high school faculty Terry's "concept of 'new white consciousness'" for the purpose of changing both how they teach and what they choose to teach.[31] Alan Hurwitz, MOREL Planning Specialist, and Valerie Snook, National Training Director for People Against Racism, designed and operated the program. According to his 2020 obituary in the New York Times, Hurwitz was also an "education director" for New Detroit, and later gained fame for developing "a crack addiction" and robbing "18 banks in three months, earning the name the 'Zombie Bandit.'" He had "no guilt about the money he stole—'He hated bankers ... .'"[32]

In line with Carmichael and Terry's views, the program focused extensively on "institutional racism," and argued that racism was not always a "deliberate, conscious action aimed specifically at oppressing black people" because even without racist motives, different outcomes could be found between races.[33] Hurwitz and Snook counseled that "those who implement [the program] ought to

---

29. Della-Dora, *Planning New Development Efforts Recommended Procedures*, 14.
30. Della-Dora, "The Culturally Disadvantaged," 470.
31. Hurwitz and Snook, "Pilot Study," 10.
32. Sandomir, "Alan Hurwitz, Teacher and Activist Who Turned to Bank Heists, Dies at 79."
33. Hurwitz and Snook, "Pilot Study," 78.

be white. Those who participate in the workshops ought to be white."[34] Among the goals of the program were for teachers to "continually evaluate their own behaviors and attitudes in terms of racism"; "actively seek to change the racist myths they believed in, and procedure practiced by, their fellow staff members"; "actively resist and try to change, by any means necessary, racist practices and policies of their schools"; and to "join with other members of the community as a whole to combat racism in institutions other than the school." Also in line with Carmichael and Terry's views was the assurance that the program was not about preparing schools for "forced integration," but rather "if the unit is successful in creating new awareness in white people, whites well might begin to actively support the concept of self-determination by blacks."

But what were the examples of "racism" that MOREL wanted to fix with this program? Many were nonsensical supposedly racist language choices. Like Terry, Snook and Hurwitz were concerned by the negative valence usually associated with words that contain "black," and the positive valence usually associated with words that contain "white." Snook and Hurwitz argued, without evidence, that these associations were enforced because "for a slave-master relationship ... the master class must feel superior." Another example they used was "the white power structure invented 'Jim Crow.' When the poor whites cried for more money to feed their hungry families they were fed 'Crow.' When the poor whites sat at the dinner table and saw their starving children they fed their children 'Crow.' The evil of racism became a staple in the daily diet of white Americans."[35] Rather than seriously contending with the actual evils of Jim Crow laws, and the ways in which these laws immiserated African Americans, Hurwitz and Snook spent more time discussing

----

34. Hurwitz and Snook, "Pilot Study," 11.
35. Hurwitz and Snook, "Pilot Study," 4.

language that they believed contributed to the sense of psychological superiority that even low-class whites have had over blacks historically. But hardly any of the language choices and behaviors Hurwitz and Snook cite as evidence of this psychological racial superiority were actually racist. "Eating Crow" had nothing to do with Jim Crow. Rather, the term was first used in print in 1850 in reference to the fact that crow (the bird) is generally considered unfit for eating.[36] They were very willing to perceive anything possible through a racial lens, writing without evidence that "since most whites believe that social welfare programs benefit black people, most whites oppose social welfare spending."[37]

Meanwhile, MOREL was well aware that integration was desired by the vast majority of African Americans. *Racism & Education* included a summary of an early 1968 "supplemental study for the National Advisory Commission on Civil Disorders," in which it "reported that 'separatism' appealed to from 5 percent to 18 percent of the Negro sample, depending on the question, with the largest appeal involving black ownership of stores and black administration of schools in Negro neighborhoods and the smallest appeal the rejection of whites as friends or in other informal contacts" and "more than three-quarters of the Negro sample indicated a clear preference for integration, representing not merely a practical wish for better material facilities, but a commitment to principles of non-discrimination and racial harmony." The study found a minority of blacks "subscribe to an emphasis on 'black consciousness,'" though the numbers were growing. The highest support for something that could be called "black consciousness" was a rather mild example, an "endorsement by 42 percent of the sample of the statement 'Negro school children should study an

---

36. World Wide Words, "Eating Crow."
37. Hurwitz and Snook, "Pilot Study," 66.

African language.'" Additionally, four out of five blacks believed "it is possible to get ahead 'in spite of prejudice and discrimination.'" And only a minority of blacks believed "that discrimination causes many Negroes to miss out on good jobs."[38] Conveniently, Hurwitz and Snook never mentioned these facts in their lessons.

While the program primarily focused on racism, Hurwitz and Snook felt the issue of power dynamics was broader, and intertwined with other identity and class differences:

 One of the most important effects racism has in white America is the creation of social and psychological patterns of dominance and submission. These same patterns can be found not only between white and black, but between men and women, the old and the young, those who have economic and political power, and those who do not. The pervasive authoritarianism necessary to justify and maintain a racial caste system, carries over into white America. The role of racial "master" itself precludes many forms of behavior: one must not deviate from acceptable (i.e. white) standards. This syndrome also prevents or hinders the possibility of behaving humanistically with other whites.[39]

Hurwitz and Snook believed it was "critical" to have their participants consider these many axes of oppression. In essence, it was a prototype of intersectional activism 20 years before Kimberly Crenshaw would coin the term "intersectionality," and eight years

---

38. Della-Dora, *Racism and Education*, 19–20.
39. Hurwitz and Snook, "Pilot Study," 65.

before the Combahee River Collective would put out a statement expressing similar ideas.[40]

Hurwitz and Snook concluded the rationale for their program by explaining, "as long as we deal exclusively with the *effects* of racism we will not have to deal at all with the *causes and practices* of racism," by which they meant language choices and societal attitudes like those above.[41] They believed that these language choices and attitudes were comparable to slavery, writing that "slavery is not a memory in the past. It is a fact of today."[42] Cementing just how thoroughly racist they believed American society to be, they claimed that "the manner of realizing achievements for many black people is to forego their dignity and individuality and adopt the white standards of success. There is, by white America's standards, no escape for a black person from his birthright caste."[43] Whether successful black people would have agreed that they had given up their "dignity and individuality," and what makes white standards of success different from black standards of success were left unclear.[44]

---

40. Columbia University Faculty, "Kimberlé Crenshaw on Intersectionality, More than Two Decades Later."

Hurwitz and Snook were hardly the first to consider these ideas though. The hugely influential Critical Theory of the Frankfurt School developed similar ideas earlier, developing from Hegel and Marx's conflict theory. See more at New Discourses: Lindsay, "The Complex Relationship Between Marxism and Wokeness."

41. Hurwitz and Snook, "Pilot Study," 7.

42. Hurwitz and Snook, "Pilot Study," 8.

43. Hurwitz and Snook, "Pilot Study," 9.

44. Hurwitz and Snook, "Pilot Study," 11.

However, later Racism Awareness Training educators would make this fully clear. Judith Katz, who will be a focus of Part 2, wrote that "individualism, hard work, objectivity, the nuclear family, a belief in progress, a written tradition, politeness, the justice system, respect for authority, delayed gratification, and planning for the future" were amongst such "aspects and assumptions of whiteness." Her material was turned into a graph published by the Smithsonian National Museum of African American History and Culture and became a major political controversy in the

MOREL's Curriculum In Action

After the predominately white Union High School in Grand Rapids Michigan had been integrated via bussing, everything went wrong. Nearly all black students desired to return to their previous school, and violence had gotten so bad the school had to be closed before Christmas vacation.[1] Racial tensions desperately needed to be solved at the school, making it the perfect testing ground for MOREL's new program.

The parents of black students requested MOREL's assistance, and the Grand Rapids Superintendent of Schools contacted MOREL to see what services could be provided. After meeting with the Board of Education, it was decided that MOREL would present to the entire high school faculty to gauge whether enough teachers would be interested in establishing a pilot study. At that presentation, MOREL staff explained that their view of racism was that "all white people growing up in this society are, inevitably, racist." They further explained that participation would lead to

---

1. Hurwitz and Snook, "Pilot Study," 12 and 143.

greater sensitivity toward racism and the development of methods to combat it. MOREL told faculty that participation was voluntary, but that participants would be paid. Despite the payment, only approximately 40 out of the 80 staff members who attended the presentation expressed interest, although 10 other teachers not present expressed interest later. The number of faculty available to meet for the first session scheduled by MOREL on January 23, 1969, was 23 (19 white and four black).[2]

The first session started relatively smoothly. MOREL instructors asked participants to name both black figures and white figures whom they considered heroes, with the agenda of showing that many white "heroes" weren't actually heroes at all, since they were slave owners (Thomas Jefferson was an example that came up in the course of the exercise). It also brought attention to the fact that whites were afraid to name black "heroes" because of the threat their philosophies represented to participants (with Malcolm X, Eldridge Cleaver, and Stokely Carmichael used as examples).[3]

In the second session, MOREL revealed that a forthcoming weekend retreat would be mandatory for continued participation. A few of the members did not react positively to the increased time demands and dropped out. Presumably in reaction to discussion of how textbooks and American society overwhelmingly focus on figures in history and in the present who happen to be white, Hurwitz and Snook recount:

 when one group member did raise the question "Why is it bad to emphasize whites" the responses were ambivalent and confused. It was further pointed out that the world is populated overwhelmingly by people

---

2.   Hurwitz and Snook, "Pilot Study," 12–14.
3.   Hurwitz and Snook, "Pilot Study," 15–16 and 62.

of color and not by white people. ... When confronted with the suggestion that *they* held racist attitudes, some reactions were highly defensive, such as "We are the liberals in the school." "We don't have to deal with ourselves, we must learn how to affect the racist on the staff." It was clear that the participants defined racism as hatred between groups or individuals and not as the assumption, on the part of whites, that white people are superior to people of color.[4]

Toward the end of the weekend retreat, MOREL staff decided that the few black participants should be segregated from the white participants, with Hurwitz and Snook explaining, "since this was a study of one's own white racism, black people could not be expected to examine themselves within this framework," "black participants had concerns and needs unique to their role as the only (four) black staff members in a total staff of 80 persons," and "white participants were 'using' black participants by questioning them instead of questioning themselves." The black participants had a mixed reaction to their segregation but ultimately went along with it.[5]

In the following session, after the retreat, MOREL staff asked participants to consider "what factors inhibit your ability to behave in an anti-racist manner?" Here answers sounded cult-like, as participants listed the problem of "nonbelievers vs. believers," and that their job as teachers was "educating, not converting." Participants also listed the "cost of commitment vs. escapism" and "friendships held higher than arguing about racism." In the next session, the "ways in which institutions created and maintained white supremacy" were examined, with participants rating

---

4. Hurwitz and Snook, "Pilot Study," 17–18.
5. Hurwitz and Snook, "Pilot Study," 21.

"government, the school and the family," as the institutions most responsible for perpetuating white supremacy.[6] According to the Cult Education Institute, one of the 10 warning signs that a person is involved in a potentially unsafe group is "increasing isolation from family and old friends unless they demonstrate an interest in the group."[7]

On March 6th, MOREL told the participants that there would be a meeting between MOREL staff and the High School Parents Association to discuss the program. Local television station WOOD-TV Grand Rapids would be televising the meeting. The participants decided they should attend as well, but when the meeting came on March 11th they were not allowed in, as it was a parents' association meeting. After MOREL explained the program, the reactions of parents were extremely negative. They accused MOREL of running "t-grouping," "sensitivity training," and "brainwashing." MOREL denied these accusations, but the parents did not accept their explanations.[8]

Indeed, the DSM-5, psychology's most recent guidebook listing diagnostic criteria for recognized psychological disorders, includes "prolonged changes in, or conscious question of, their identity" as a result of "intense coercive persuasion (e.g., brainwashing, thought reform ...)" as "Other Specified Dissociative Disorder" if it causes "clinically significant distress" (such as the "anxiety" MOREL staff themselves identified as experiencing).[9] Thus, it appears that the coercive methods used by MOREL to change the identities of their participants to that of a "new white consciousness," creating significant anxiety in the process, could legitimately and

---

6. Hurwitz and Snook, "Pilot Study," 22–25.
7. Ross, "Ten Signs of a Potentially Unsafe Group/Leader."
8. Hurwitz and Snook, "Pilot Study," 25.
9. American Psychiatric Association, *Diagnostic and Statistical Manual of Mental Disorders*, 306.

scientifically be interpreted as brainwashing to instill a psychological disorder.

During the next week's meeting, no program progress was made. Instead, "the entire meeting was spent discussing the meeting with the Parents Association and possible responses. ... It was also felt by many participants that the [High School Parents Association] was racist in that it opposed combating racism, that it was preoccupied with nonexistent 'black racism' and its [school board] candidates were taking a clear anti-bussing stand in the election." It was decided that the group would hold a press conference to support the MOREL program.[10]

All the local newspapers and many of the radio and television stations attended the press conference. However, the group's statement gave no indication that MOREL was teaching deeply unusual and divisive views on race. At no point was it mentioned that MOREL and People Against Racism considered all whites to be racist, that they considered the word "crow" or any other word to be racist, that Stokely Carmichael inspired their thinking about race relations, or that they considered all of American society to be racist. Instead, they made broadly agreeable statements such as "our primary concern has been to create an atmosphere of better understanding among the students and staff at the High School. This better understanding can best be accomplished by dealing directly with the problem of white racism, its attitudes and behavior. If we remain silent on the issue of racism, we do nothing more than allow racism to be perpetuated." And "we believe that any efforts to combat racism can only have a positive affect [sic] on our community."[11]

This example remains emblematic of how these activities are

---

10. Hurwitz and Snook, "Pilot Study," 27.
11. Hurwitz and Snook, "Pilot Study," 28–31.

defended today.[12] Their response is an example of what's known as a "Motte & Bailey" rhetorical strategy. A logical fallacy, the "Motte" refers to a modest position that is relatively easy to defend, while the "Bailey" is the more controversial position. Rather than trying to defend this controversial position, when one is challenged while trying to advance the Bailey, they will instead pretend to have been arguing for the Motte.[13] In its response, MOREL suggested that its teachings were merely concerned with fostering a "better understanding" between students and teachers of different racial backgrounds (Motte), while in reality, MOREL was promulgating a conception of racism that conflicted with the beliefs of the vast majority of Americans (Bailey). MOREL knew that their understanding of racism was in a tiny minority, and must have known that its viewpoints would not be accepted by the general public (at least not at this time in history). Rather than informing the public directly of their program's radical agenda, MOREL focused on the semantic fact that they were an "anti-racist" organization, running an "anti-racist" program, and that "efforts to combat racism" are good. Only those with inside knowledge understood that "anti-racist" meant something different to MOREL than to almost everyone else, and that their "efforts to combat racism" involved working to eventually tear down all American institutions. Yet, to avoid controversy, they hid those facts. What reasonable person could oppose "anti-racism?"

The final work session of Hurwitz and Snook's program involved a presentation to non-participating faculty. Only six out of a possible 60 people chose to attend. Clearly the pilot program was overwhelmingly a failure, but it would have an impact on most of its

---

12. For more see Lindsay, "Stealing the Motte."

13. Boudry and Braeckman, "Immunizing Strategies and Epistemic Defense Mechanisms," 145–61.

participants. Much like the internal self-examination at MOREL, on a post-program evaluation, one participant noted that they were more anxious afterward. Possibly fitting the DSM-5 criteria for "Other Specified Dissociative Disorder," some participants also claimed that the program "created stress and frustration," which led them to withdraw from some individuals and created an uneasy relationship between themselves and fellow staff members. One participant even noted that their participation led to their family being harassed by phone calls and neighbors, presumably after the news debacle. When asked what methods participants would use to deal with mental blocks around acknowledging their racism, one answered that they would "ignore friends."[14] Although Hurwitz and Snook claimed the unit was "not intended to create guilt complexes in whites" and "we do not intend to promote self-flagellation," that appeared to be the effect.[15]

On the "positive" side, a participant decided that they would raise their children as anti-racists, and 15 out of 17 respondents gave an A or a B on an A through E scale of "how much I learned about my own racism" and "how much I learned about societal/institutional racism." Written responses included: "I have become much more aware. At first I could not accept the concept of white racism, now I see the results of such"; "I feel that I have come a long way from our first session in my commitment to overcome racist tendencies in myself that I never knew existed"; and "my entire basic attitude changed. I had not been committed to activity seeking change until participation in MOREL."[16]

Hurwitz and Snook ended their study with ideas for what future programs should attempt, given what they learned from their

---

14. Hurwitz and Snook, "Pilot Study," 33–57.
15. Hurwitz and Snook, "Pilot Study," 11.
16. Hurwitz and Snook, "Pilot Study," 33–57.

experience. One of the most important findings was that they needed to slowly and methodically ease people into understanding their message:

> The goals of white people who have not previously been involved in racially liberating experiences will be racist. The racist characteristics of their goals may range from open rejection of black people to paternalistic interests in the affairs of black America. Seeking resolution of goal conflict early in a training experience is an inhibiting force. Programs designed to create anti-racist behavior in white school personnel must recognize that the overwhelming majority of white people in our society are not able to deal with racism until such a time as they have had sufficient knowledge to create a new frame of reference for themselves. White people must begin to understand what it means to be white in a racist society.[17]

And:

> It is critical to the long range success of any anti-racist training program that the people participating develop the ability to be self-directing and continually searching in their efforts. As rapidly as the group displays an ability to deal honestly with racism and "emerging leadership" comes to the fore, the leader should become less directing and more facilitating for group activity. This withdrawal from directing to facilitating behavior by the leaders should begin to

---

17. Hurwitz and Snook, "Pilot Study," 60.

occur only after the group has demonstrated that it is really committed to anti-racism and not just to some paternalistic endeavors that they see as being done in [sic] behalf of the black community. The efforts that participants make in the direction of assuming leadership for the group or oneself should be highly supported by trainers.[18]

They also found that their program could do psychological and social harm, but believed that this was a sign of success:

If effective, anti-racist training programs will create anti-social behaviors. This is because the "normal" patterns of social behavior in our society currently are racist. White people have countless experiences throughout their lives in learning more sophisticated forms of socially acceptable racist behavior. One of the major difficulties faced in having an effective anti-racist training program is the fact that many of the outcomes will be anti-social by the prevailing white norm. Examples are:

(1) refusing to teach that Lincoln was the "great emanicipator" [sic]

(2) presenting revolutionary figures such as Malcolm X, Eldridge Cleaver, and Stokley [sic] Carmichael as positive models

(3) investigating, with students, the racism that pervades the institutions of white America

(4) dealing openly with the racism of American

---

18. Hurwitz and Snook, "Pilot Study," 72.

imperialism in reviewing past and current foreign relations and policies. ...

Programs designed to resolve the racial crisis must develop with the foresight that difficulties will be encountered by the participants who will be exhibiting anti-social behaviors, which means attempts to examine and change what it means to be white.[19]

The results of their study also led them to refine how they believed their ideas could be best framed for acceptance:

 Emphasis should be placed on the liberating dynamic of anti-racist behavior as opposed to discussing "dire consequences." In a discussion of an individual's ability to challenge the racist position of other staff members it should be strongly emphasized that losing the so-called "friendship" of such people is a liberating, not a negative, result. Further, it is important to stress the need for white people to exhibit anti-racist behavior so other "fence-sitting" whites will be encouraged to do the same.[20]

And:

 Efforts must be made to minimize the resistance of the target population. However, efforts to reduce resistance cannot be made at the cost of sacrificing the anti-racist nature of the activity. Propaganda that

19. Hurwitz and Snook, "Pilot Study," 60–61.
20. Hurwitz and Snook, "Pilot Study," 69.

highlights the mass appeal aspects of the anti-racist efforts should constantly be made available to the target population. Those activities and comments that enable people to be supported in their desire to change the status quo should be pursued throughout the strategy.[21]

They also recommended, "a set of anti-racist behaviors that school personnel may want to use can range from the incorporation of a black studies program into the curriculum to militant interference with school practices and policies that perpetuate white supremist attitudes and behaviors."[22]

But perhaps most important for future iterations of anti-racist programming was what Hurwitz and Snook considered the essential tool for opposing racism:

> One activity that is common to all these models is an investigation of personal racism. This self-examination must be ongoing throughout training experience and beyond. Meaningful commitment and resulting action to combat racism are products of personal analyses and consequent changes in knowledge, behavior, and attitudes.
>
> "Active" anti-racist behavior is the point at which an individual actively and consciously pursues those activities which will eliminate the racist nature of American society. Movement toward active anti-racist behavior involves being fully aware of what attitudes one holds as an individual. How did I acquire those

21. Hurwitz and Snook, "Pilot Study," 71.
22. Hurwitz and Snook, "Pilot Study," 69.

attitudes? How do I acquire a very different set of attitudes? How well am I developing both new attitudes and new behaviors?[23]

Bidol's curriculum would be designed around that investigation of personal racism.

.

---

23. Hurwitz and Snook, "Pilot Study," 75.

The Legitimization of Carmichael's Radicalism

In January 1970, the United States Commission on Civil Rights published the first volume of *Racism In America and How to Combat It*, entitled *The Nature of Racism*. The essay was written by Anthony Downs, a white man who had been a consultant to the Kerner Commission, the RAND Corporation, the Urban Institute, the Brookings Institution, and the Ford Foundation.[1] Starting in 1969, the Ford Foundation had been funding "black studies" departments at universities that spread black separatist ideas.[2]

Downs himself was not a particularly radical figure. Although clearly left-leaning, working with the left-wing Ford and Brookings, he was an economist who contributed to the "public choice" school of economics, typically associated with right-of-center views.[3] But his essay was more radical than his background suggests, as it

1. U.S. Commission on Civil Rights, *Racism in America and How to Combat It*, preface.
2. Stevens, "Book Reveals Influence of White Philanthropy on Founding and Future of Black Studies."
3. Downs, *An Economic Theory of Democracy*.

effectively copied and pasted large sections of Stokely Carmichael's *Black Power* without attributing Downs' views to Carmichael.

In light of the failure of the previous Kerner Commission report to explicitly define racism, this essay served as a follow-up. Like Carmichael, Downs falsely claimed that many people could not clearly define racism, and he used that as grounds to introduce his own definition: "any attitude, action, or institutional structure which subordinates a person or group because of his or their skin color." Downs' essay also featured the same split of "overt" versus "institutional" racism, defining them nearly exactly as Carmichael did. These definitions allowed Downs to claim that "the separation of the races is not racism unless it leads to or involves subordination."

However, despite parroting large volumes of Carmichael's ideas, Downs' essay never quite reached the same levels of radicalism as *Black Power* did, and it included several caveats that tempered its positions. For example, clarifying that, although separation of the races alone was not sufficient to be called racism, "separation of groups is one of the oldest and most widespread devices for subordination" and that it would be racist if "black students forced other black students to live in a specific dormitory."[4] Even though Downs defined "institutional subordination" in the same way Carmichael defined "institutional racism," there wasn't a hint of Marxism in Downs' writing. For Downs, an act of overt racism must always appear at some point before institutional subordination is created.[5]

Expressing radical ideas in a more tempered manner—the way Robert Terry and MOREL did—Downs still considered most white Americans "unintentional racists" for participating in an institutionally racist system. But unlike Terry and MOREL, he

---

4. U.S. Commission on Civil Rights, *Racism in America and How to Combat It*, 5.
5. U.S. Commission on Civil Rights, *Racism in America and How to Combat It*, 16.

clarified it would be both "wrong and harmful to consider persons who support institutional subordination as 'racists' in the same sense as those who practice overt racism."[6]

The suggestions for combating racism would also be milder than Downs' intellectual predecessors. In the preface, Otto Kerner wrote that he "enthusiastically endorse[d] the strategies suggested in this paper."[7] Downs, like Martin Luther King Jr., would suggest developing "legislative and other programs which simultaneously provide benefits for significant parts of the white majority and for deprived or other members of non-white minority groups, so it will be in the immediate interest of the former to support programs which aid the latter." In essence, he was describing colorblind anti-poverty programs. Downs was even careful to clarify that:

 it is vital that society avoid creating low-income minority group neighborhoods that are almost totally dependent upon direct public expenditures aimed at self-maintenance, rather than at producing services consumed by society as a whole. Such a position of primarily nonproductive dependency discourages initiative among residents, reinforces their feelings of inadequacy and inferiority, results in a very low standard of living because of legislative economizing, and tends to confirm existing stereotypes that the residents are lazy and incompetent. It could even lead to a permanent publicly maintained "underclass" in slum areas differentiated by dependency, location, and color.[8]

6. U.S. Commission on Civil Rights, *Racism in America and How to Combat It,* 17.
7. U.S. Commission on Civil Rights, *Racism in America and How to Combat It,* 1.
8. U.S. Commission on Civil Rights, *Racism in America and How to Combat It,* 33.

But Downs also made suggestions that would enable the spread of the more radical vision of his contemporaries. He argued in favor of "Black Nationalism" and stronger black self-identification with race, and also that "whites must thoroughly examine their own behavior in order to uncover all the subtle and unconscious forms of racism embedded in it."[9]

Downs' essay was controversial within the Commission on Civil Rights. A joint statement by the commissioners at the end of the publication clarified, "the commission is publishing this essay as a challenge to all thoughtful and concerned Americans. We claim no ultimate wisdom." The Vice Chairman of the Commission stated, "to accuse the United States of America of being a 'racist' society is inaccurate and misleading." Directly opposing the notion that minorities cannot be racist without societal power, he wrote, "I believe that it is paternalism of the worst sort to condemn one type of racism and to condone the other. I am opposed to black racism, white racism, and racism in any form wherever it is found. I believe that the great majority of the American people are also opposed to racism in all its forms." Another one of the commissioners wrote that Downs' essay differed from the Commission's previous "exhaustive and factual" empirical studies, and he was "not sure that [the essay's publication] is a good move."[10]

In practice, despite Downs translating Carmichael into less radical, more nuanced language, as it was published by a government office, the essay served to stamp legitimacy onto his less credible and more radical contemporaries. Downs' paper was later

---

9. U.S. Commission on Civil Rights, *Racism in America and How to Combat It*, 28 and 26.
10. U.S. Commission on Civil Rights, *Racism in America and How to Combat It*, 40–42.

widely cited by those attempting to push the "Power + Prejudice" redefinition.[11]

---

11. For one important example, see Katz, *White Awareness. White Awareness* will be discussed in depth in Part 2.

New Detroit Publishes Pat Bidol:
Enter "Power • Prejudice"

By late 1969, New Detroit had established itself into four distinct roles:

1. "Advocacy. New Detroit shall forthrightly and consistently be prepared to adopt both popular and unpopular positions on behalf of necessary social changes."
2. "Precept and Example. New Detroit shall attempt to be a pacesetter to encourage new patterns of social action and attitude."
3. "Catalytic Agent. New Detroit shall attempt to make existing institutions more responsive to the needs of black and other minorities, and to aid in the community creation of institutions where none exist to take care of identified needs."
4. "Provider of Resources. New Detroit shall seek to procure the necessary and most appropriate resources to meet its goals. These resources shall include human

resources and the influence of the Board, as well as financial and other material resources."

Pat Bidol's project fit all of these roles and built on the work that the Speakers' Bureau was already executing, which by October 1969, had utilized "150 active volunteers and reached some 188,000 people."[1]

Bidol first tested her curriculum by teaching it as a 10-week elective for juniors and seniors in the Greater Metropolitan Detroit Area.[2] Upon completion, in 1970, New Detroit, Inc. published "Developing New Perspectives on Race: An Innovative Multi-Media Social Studies Curriculum in Race Relations for the Secondary Level." New Detroit was aware that its brand would "lend credibility and prestige" to Bidol's curriculum.[3] In the acknowledgments, Bidol thanked "Dr. Delmo Della-Dora," the "Detroit Industrial Mission," "Robert W. Terry," and "Jo-Ann Terry," among others.[4] As Della-Dora had been a deputy superintendent in Wayne County, Michigan, it is likely that he and Bidol had previously worked together.[5] Terry was specifically given credit for the concept of "New White Consciousness," which, Bidol wrote, "provided for confused white liberals and conservatives a new meaningful alternative when it was crucially needed."[6]

Bidol explained the purpose of her curriculum as such:

 Six years ago, the author believed the problem of racial injustice would be solved if the moral conscience of

---

1. New Detroit, "A New Detroit Assessment."
2. Bidol, *Developing New Perspectives on Race*, 1.
3. Doss, "Recommendations to the Board of Trustees," 35.
4. Bidol, *Developing New Perspectives on Race*, Acknowledgements.
5. Della-Dora, "The Culturally Disadvantaged," 467.
6. Bidol, *Developing New Perspectives on Race*, Acknowledgements.

the nation could be awakened, for example, that if all our laws dealing with equality would be enforced, we would create a just society. Now it is clear that the problem is one of white racism and that its profound effects can undermine the enforcement of even moral laws. Removal of its effects must begin with achievement of an understanding of racism as it is found throughout our society. The goal of the course is to create within the student an awareness of white racism and to enable him to identify its forms within the culture, institutions, and individual behaviors of our society.[7]

Bidol cited an essay published by MOREL that Hurwitz and Snook had previously utilized in their curriculum to teach people that all of American society was racist. She appeared to agree in full with its view:

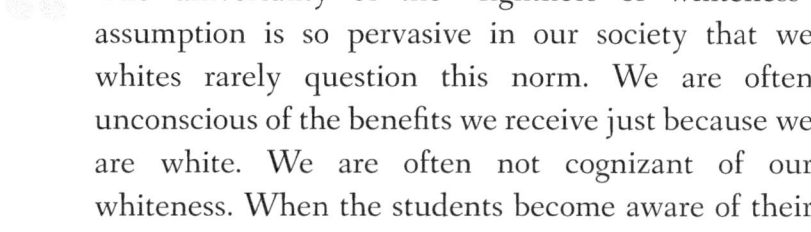

The universality of the "rightness of whiteness" assumption is so pervasive in our society that we whites rarely question this norm. We are often unconscious of the benefits we receive just because we are white. We are often not cognizant of our whiteness. When the students become aware of their whiteness and realize the implications of what it means to be white in a white racist society, they often become threatened.

The teacher must be able to accept the emotions of the students and assist the students to accept their emotions. By assisting the students in releasing their

---

7. Bidol, *Developing New Perspectives on Race*, 1.

emotions, the teacher will facilitate increasing their ability to understand the content of the units and to integrate that content themselves.[8]

As Hurwitz and Snook suggested, "as the unit progresses, the role of the teacher shifts from 'leader' to 'resource person'" and "self-examination and self-evaluation by the group must be an integral part of the learning process. If the students feel that they are here to learn, instead of being 'taught from on high', they will honestly and critically share in the responsibility of evaluating."[9]

The curriculum was split into five units. The first was "White Awareness—focusing on the historical, psychological, and sociological aspects of whiteness in America." The second was "Prejudice and Racism—focusing on the differences between prejudice and racism." That unit would include Bidol's definition list and the first use of "Power + Prejudice." The third was "Institutional Racism." The fourth was "Black America—exposing the students to the fundamental realities of black American history and contemporary culture." The fifth was "New White America—exploring what it means to be an anti-racist white in a white racist society."

The unit on white awareness was recommended to last two-and-a-half to three weeks. It featured a number of the same exercises that Hurwitz and Snook used, and it also asked students to read "The Rightness of Whiteness" essay on cultural racism published by MOREL.[10] Notably, outside the readings, the unit never tells the students outright what views they should hold; rather, it included numerous exercises intended to prime the students to realize that

---

8. Bidol, *Developing New Perspectives on Race*, 3.
9. Bidol, *Developing New Perspectives on Race*, 3–4.
10. Bidol, *Developing New Perspectives on Race*, 31.

they had unconsciously been viewing black people and things associated with black people negatively, and white people and things associated with white people positively. This would allegedly explain, for example, why they viewed "riots" and the "ghetto" negatively while they viewed the "American Revolution of 1776" and the "suburbs" positively, implying that value judgments between those things stemmed only from "schooling" or "family norms," not from any objective difference.[11] That and other exercises don't list any predetermined desired outcomes, but it is easy to imagine the social pressure that participants must have felt to avoid vocally challenging the exercises' unmistakably implied intent: to convince participants to adopt Bidol's bizarre conception of race. Ironically, one exercise asked students to list the "ideals of American society" and how the freedoms associated with these ideals were disproportionately granted to white people versus black people; freedom of speech was offered as an example, with the note that "if a [black] person gets too radical and/or inflammatory, he often is not allowed to speak."[12] Ironically, today it seems it's more often people who believe in "Power + Prejudice" and its associated views on racism who would deny free speech to those who disagree with them.[13]

The second unit on prejudice and racism began by asking students to define the key words "prejudice" and "racism." One of the leading questions used to guide students towards Bidol's "Power + Prejudice" definition was to "distinguish between prejudice and racism." The problem for Bidol was that the most common

---

11. Bidol, *Developing New Perspectives on Race*, 19.
12. Bidol, *Developing New Perspectives on Race*, 27.
13. Such as OnlyBlackGirl, who argued that since "the dictionary is outdated and based on white male opinions," those arguing for the validity of the dictionary definition "need to log off" social media and "take this L with you." OnlyBlackGirl, "Your Dictionary Definition of Racism Is Outdated Trash."

dictionary definition of racism at the time was prejudice along racial lines. But since Carmichael had defined "subordination" and "control" as necessary elements for institutional racism, Bidol needed to ask students to try to differentiate racism from prejudice if they were to ultimately accept her "Power + Prejudice" definition. This was in line with Kurt Lewin's teaching that "an individual will believe facts he himself has discovered in the same way that he believes in himself." Lewin and NTL understood that students coming to a conclusion themselves (even if they were manipulated) meant "he cannot challenge [findings] as being inadequate or impute any bias to the finder. If others have found the same thing at the same time, all must recognize—necessarily—that they had been mistaken."[14]

   To accomplish this, Bidol picked the *Random House Dictionary of the English Language* (1967) to cite in her definition list, an outdated outlier that didn't include racial prejudice, which would make it more difficult for students to accept the most common definition. This was a particularly suspicious choice as the more recent Random House dictionary edition, released in 1968, conformed more closely to other dictionaries' definitions of the word, adding "hatred or intolerance of another race or other races."[15]

---

14. Bradford, *National Training Laboratories*, Appendix 1.

15. 1967 "racism" entry: "1. the belief that human races have distinctive make-ups that determine their respective cultures, usually involving the idea that one's own race is superior and has the right to rule others. 2. a policy of enforcing such asserted rights. 3. a system of government and society based upon it." *Random House Dictionary of the English Language*, 1967, "racism."

   1968 "racism" entry: "1. a doctrine that inherent differences among the various human races determine cultural or individual achievement, usually involving the idea that one's own race is superior. 2. a policy, government, etc. based on such a doctrine. 3. hatred or intolerance of another race or races." *Random House Dictionary of the English Language*, 1968, "racism."

   In addition to the adding "hatred or intolerance of another race or races," it's interesting to note that the 1968 definition struck "and has the right to rule others"

Bidol also included Terry's definition from *For Whites Only* and a definition from Dr. Joel Kovel that "racism is a set of beliefs whose structure arises from the deepest levels of our lives—from the fabric of assumptions we make about the world, ourselves, and others, and from the patterns of our fundamental social activities"—a definition so vague that one could replace racism with "philosophy," "religion," or hundreds of other words and it would still make sense. However, it's important to note that at this stage, nothing in the curriculum stipulates that students *must* come to accept Bidol's "Power + Prejudice" definition; rather, students were directed to discuss and come to their own conclusions on how to distinguish between "prejudice" and "racism," although Bidol's solution was heavily implied. That would not be the case in future similar curricula.[16]

So why did Bidol coin her definition? It should be clear by now that, as a follower of Carmichael and those influenced by him in Detroit, Bidol would come to this view. But she explained it more explicitly a few years later in her *Mini Lecture on Differences Between Prejudice and Racism:*

> As the momentum of the [civil rights] movement moved into the sixties, liberal white activists were being told that if they were really serious about this issue they could not continue to try to save black communities but must face the necessity of going back into their own white communities and working with

---

from definition one and entirely struck 1967's third definition. The third definition from the 1967 version was much closer to Carmichael's "institutional racism" in *Black Power*, which was also published in 1967. Yet within just one year, Random House appears to have realized that the definition wasn't accurate and removed it. Despite this removal, Racism Awareness Training would continue to cite the idiosyncratic 1967 definition for some time.

16. Judith Katz, who wrote a nearly identical curriculum to Bidol's, made this change and will be discussed further in Part 2.

white folks, where the problem really was. This constituted new data which while previously unknown, was relevant to this situation. As a consequence of this new data many liberal whites deserted the movement, becoming suddenly prejudiced negatively toward a previously positively viewed activity. The new data was regarded as a false analysis, and used as a rationale to support leaving the movement. (Many of my associates of those early years question my continued involvement—they who were willing to die for the revolution were not willing to live to work for it.) Thus one can readily see how prejudice is always behaviorally negative and can be damaging to large numbers of people.[17]

This information about whites being told to go back to the white community confirms that Bidol was either involved with the Student Nonviolent Coordinating Committee or another Carmichael-influenced movement. The fact that Bidol's "associates" became prejudiced against SNCC or the black separatist movement is far from surprising, given that these movements were excommunicating them based solely on their skin color. Yet Bidol never seemed to consider that it may have been the movement she was a part of that was racist and problematic. According to the Cult Education Institute "the group/leader is always right" is one of the 10 warning signs of a potentially unsafe group.[18]

Bidol continued with her views on racism:

---

17. Bidol, *The Effects of Racism Awareness Training on the Professional Staff of an Education Association*, 124.
18. Ross, "Ten Signs of a Potentially Unsafe Group/Leader."

> Racism, according to the *Random House Dictionary of the English Language,* 1967 is defined as 1. A belief that human races have distinctive characteristics that determine their respective cultures, usually involving the idea that one's own race is superior and has the right to rule others. 2. A policy enforcing such assorted rights and 3. A system of government and society based on it. Racism in the United States then is the perpetuation of the belief in the superiority and privileges of the white race.
>
> Therefore, if you live in a society in which the racial prejudice of the majority group is reinforced by the culture and institutions of that society then racial prejudice becomes racism. Consequently, in the United States only whites can be racists since at present, whites dominate and control the institutions of our society which create our cultural norms and values.[19]

It's important to recognize the logical leaps Bidol makes to support her claims. Even putting aside that the entry in the 1967 Random House dictionary was an outlier, and that by 1968 it had already been updated to the more common definition, only the 1967 edition's third definition of "a system of government and society" would suggest that racism could flow in only one direction. The first two more common uses cannot be interpreted that way. If the second or third definition is selected, then racism is more like slavery, South African apartheid, or Jim Crow in that "belief" isn't necessarily relevant, just clearly racially discriminatory policies. Not

---

19. Bidol, The Effects of Racism Awareness Training on the Professional Staff of an Education Association, 124-125.

one of the three definitions taken alone can support the notion that racism in America can only be "the perpetuation of the belief in the superiority of the white race."[20]

Even if racism in America were only belief in the superiority of the white race, it would still not necessarily mean that "the racial prejudice of the majority group is reinforced by the culture and institutions." That assertion is an empirical claim, and it is not clear from the evidence that the majority of American whites were prejudiced (though certainly significantly more of them were prejudiced than are today), nor was it clear that a sufficient amount of American culture and institutions were still reinforcing such prejudice—that is unless you incorrectly believe that disliking Stokely Carmichael and black separatism, or using phrases like "eating Crow," or the use of "black" the color in a negative way are examples of prejudice against African Americans.

Finally, even if that were the case, it's utterly unclear how that would mean "in the United States only whites can be racists." America is not a homogenous society, but rather a collection of local communities—many of them predominantly black. Surely Bidol would not claim that only blacks can be racist in a black neighborhood, at a predominately black school, or in a black-led company. Activists today often try to defend the "Power + Prejudice" definition against this and similar counter-arguments by saying that they are referring to American society as a whole. But these activists rarely explain why this big-picture perspective is the only correct way to study the United States; it is necessarily reductionist, and it appears to be motivated more by a desire to defend the redefinition than to find the most effective framework for

---

20. This is how a dictionary works; it does not assert that all three definitions are used simultaneously in any given use of the word "racism." In fact, by separating the definitions, it explicitly lays out different possibilities for how a word might be used.

studying racism.[21] Regardless, Bidol never provided such an explanation.

Bidol finishes her derivation of "Power + Prejudice" by stating:

> This is not to say that blacks and/or other Third World peoples could not be racists, that they do not have the capacity to hate, to develop and enforce anti-white norms and standards. To so state would be dehumanizing and racist. The point is that in the U.S. at this time, blacks and other Third World peoples do not have access to the power to enforce such prejudicial concepts. Therefore, they cannot by definition, be racists. Racism equals prejudice plus power.[22]

It is not true that blacks or "Third World peoples" (by which Bidol means those outside the US, Europe, or the Soviet Union, "all of whom have at one time or another been under the domination of the First World") do not have the power to enforce their prejudice in the United States. Granted, they certainly are not able to on the same scale—and white racism in America has always been worse—but any black business owner or black person working in a store that chooses to discriminate against customers of another race has enough power to enforce their prejudice. A black teacher, professor, or principal who might choose to discriminate against students of another race has enough power to enforce their prejudice. A black social club that excludes other races has enough power to enforce their prejudice (see SNCC). A black person who chooses to commit

---

21. See Robin DiAngelo asserting this position: DiAngelo, "Deconstructing White Privilege with Robin DiAngelo."
22. Bidol, "The Effects of Racism Awareness Training on the Professional Staff of an Education Association," 125.

a hate crime against a person of another race has enough power to enforce their prejudice. The list could go on endlessly. It doesn't take a lot of power to enforce prejudice.

While never explicitly stated by Bidol, she may have believed that her "Power + Prejudice" definition would help students focus on the true problem of white racism rather than allowing them to be distracted by what Hurwitz and Snook called "nonexistent black racism."[23]

Next in the curriculum was the relatively short unit on institutional racism. Taking Robert Terry's position, Bidol believed that not only were all American institutions racist, but that this meant that all white individuals are racist:

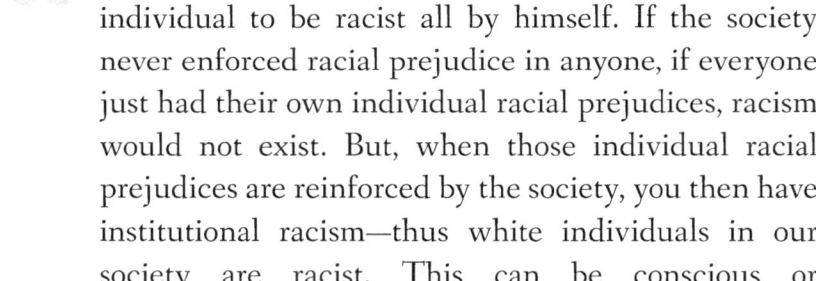

> In our society it would be very difficult for any individual to be racist all by himself. If the society never enforced racial prejudice in anyone, if everyone just had their own individual racial prejudices, racism would not exist. But, when those individual racial prejudices are reinforced by the society, you then have institutional racism—thus white individuals in our society are racist. This can be conscious or unconscious. If a white person is totally free of all conscious racial prejudices, he remains, in our society, a racist. He receives benefits distributed by a white racist society through its institutions.
>
> It is essential for whites to recognize that most of these racist benefits now occur automatically, unconsciously, covertly and unintentionally. Individual whites do not have to consciously decide to oppress black and other Third World peoples in order

---

23. Hurwitz and Snook, "Pilot Study," 27.

to be a racist. The societal arrangements of our culture, based on 'assumed' white superiority, make it impossible for whites to not receive benefits. Many of these benefits are so deeply imbedded [sic] in the matrix of our white being, individually and collectively, that it is very difficult to become aware of them. Whites must simply accept the fact in our society they are racists.[24]

But it's not the case that a white racist society necessarily confers benefits to whites. While clearly anti-black racism is worse for blacks, it can also be bad for both. Less discrimination and prejudice make a society wealthier and more productive as a whole. White people—indeed all people—in a racist society are deprived of the skills and knowledge of black people, who would otherwise flow freely within the economy toward their most productive uses as incentivized by market forces. White people would also be deprived of the friendship of blacks. It's not clear why the supposed psychological benefits from whites considering themselves superior, even if they could be proven to exist, would outweigh the economic and social negatives of racism. Even if it were the case that all whites in a white racist society received benefits, Bidol provides no justification for why that means all white individuals are racist—she simply asserts that it is true.

Additionally, while under Bidol's definition it is true that individual racial prejudice alone can't create racism, that argument shows how unproductive her definition of racism was. Prejudice along racial lines is a problem distinct from other forms of prejudice, and even if racism has largely been cleansed from American

---

24. Bidol, "The Effects of Racism Awareness Training on the Professional Staff of an Education Association," 128.

institutions, each individual act of racism is still a problem. Bidol's definition would deprive society of a word to encapsulate that concept and a tool to better discuss it and combat it.[25]

The "Unit on Black America" instructed students to read an essay or view a film by Stokely Carmichael. It also sought to "expose the students to current expressions of Black Power, especially as evidenced in Detroit," with a particular focus on the Black Panthers.[26]

The final "Unit on New White America" explicitly taught students the views of Robert Terry, requiring them to read *For Whites Only*. For the first time, it asked students to look at conservative views on race, asking students to interview "radical" political thinkers, "liberal" political thinkers, and "conservative" political thinkers to gain an understanding of their views. This seems like an innocent assignment, except that its recommendations for conservative organizations included the "John Birch Society" at best and the "United Klans of America" at worst. The list did not

---

25. Bidol also showed she believed that communism was one of the proper solutions for racism, though not explicitly using that word: "Another major pitfall is the whole concept of 'helping' those whom we have systematically repressed. 'Helping' implies that we whites are in control of the resources, and that we will decide who gets what and how much. We need to begin to develop a concept of sharing rather than helping. Sharing implies that we all are going to somehow share control of our resources and see to it that they are used in the direction of guaranteeing mutual survival." Bidol, "Mini-Lecture on Differences Between Prejudice and Racism."

There's nothing wrong with sharing, of course, except when sharing isn't actually sharing, but is a "need" or coerced, at which point it's taking. The word "somehow" allows Bidol to weasel out of needing to explain how that shared resource control would work, which historically has been the most difficult part of communist economies. Moreover, Bidol provides no reason for why it's wrong that individuals who produce things of value for others and acquire resources in exchange ought to feel that it's wrong for them to control the resources that are the fruits of their labor. Rather than taking resources from productive people to be shared, obstacles in the way of black people should be removed so that they have the entrepreneurial means to acquire resource control of their own.

26. Bidol, *Developing New Perspectives on Race*, 55–57.

include a single mainstream conservative organization, instead presenting an actively racist fringe group as if it represented mainstream conservative thought. On the radical side, it recommended students interview Frank Joyce. The unit also expanded the discussion of white America's sins beyond black America, adding in focus on Native Americans, Mexican Americans, and America's role in "Indochina."

Although it would take time to catch on in the wider world, Bidol's redefinition spread quickly within her community.

Pat Bidol's Friends Adopt
Her View

The same year that Bidol's curriculum was first published, Delmo Della-Dora wrote his own essay defending the redefinition titled "Racism and Prejudice: How Did We Get This Way?" It was included in *What Curriculum Leaders Can Do About Racism,* published by New Detroit, Inc. and Michigan Education Associates (MEA), a public school employees union and the third largest teachers and school personnel union in the United States.[1]

---

1. Della-Dora, "Racism and Prejudice," 1.

Despite attempts, research was not able to turn up the full copy of this book, though it was able to turn up a complete scan of the chapter at the University of Michigan library. That scan attributes publishing to Michigan Education Associates, but other sources, including the Michigan Education Association's Multi-Ethnic Handbook (to be discussed in Part 2), cite the book as being published by New Detroit, Inc. Additionally, the publication month of this book was unable to be confirmed. Thus it is theoretically possible the "Power + Prejudice" redefinition was first published here rather than by Bidol. However, other secondary sources attribute the redefinition to Bidol. See Sivanandan, "RAT and the Degradation of Black Struggle," 149.

MEA also promotes its affiliation with the National Education Association, the largest labor union in the United States.[2]

Della-Dora attempted to spread the "Power + Prejudice" redefinition among educators, writing, "when you combine power with racial discrimination, the result is racism. For all practical purposes, therefore, 'racism' and 'white racism' mean the same thing."[3] Della-Dora had become even more radicalized since his previous writing on the topic—now adopting the view, shared by his self-described anti-racist colleagues, that all whites are racist and contribute to racism unless they adopt the Terry/Carmichael position:

> The nature of our society today is such that every white person (and many black people) are contributing to racism daily. A few white people are working against it at various times. There is no "neutral" or middle ground—except in the sheltered imagination of some well-meaning whites. ... If no black people, or only a few, are employed in your school or district and you have not continually worked to change this condition, you're helping to maintain it. ... Harsh as it may sound, all white people in our country are racists in the sense that they are the majority, they collectively control all major institutions, and—unless they work constantly to change discriminatory practices—are helping maintain our society's racist practices.[4]

2.   Michigan Education Association, "About Us."
3.   Della-Dora, "Racism and Prejudice," 1.
4.   Della-Dora, "Racism and Prejudice," 1-2.

Della-Dora also believed that "we have all been infected with racism. That doesn't excuse anyone but it does mean that we have to be aware of our disease, if we are to cure it rather than spread it further."[5] This equation of white racism with a literal psychological disease would be expanded upon by new followers of the ideology in the mid-1970s.[6]

Terry also integrated Bidol's redefinition into his work, writing in his December 1970 paper "New Whites—Justice and Racism" that "no individual can be racist in isolation. He must be able to translate his racial prejudice into societal forms that perpetuate a particular color group's advantages over another color group. ... Although blacks can in our society be prejudiced—misjudge a particular situation because of scanty data (a phenomenon that happens less frequently than I originally thought)—blacks cannot be racist in America in 1970 regardless of their views—prejudiced or not."[7]

Terry built on Bidol's ideas to say that racism wasn't just bigotry either: "As with racial prejudice, elimination of racial bigotry, by itself, would not guarantee the elimination of racism. Frequently, racist and bigot are confused and only bigots, the confusion implies, should be called racist. ... non-bigots also can be and are racist if they benefit from white privilege and passively let power, structure and culture protect that privilege." This means, again, at the very least, that refusing to accept Terry's radical views on dismantling America's structure and culture makes one racist. At the very most, it also means that all whites are necessarily racist, with Terry clarifying that "new whites need not be afraid to admit they are racists because it's true. New whites need not be afraid to live in the

---

5. Della-Dora, "Racism and Prejudice," 3.
6. This will be discussed further in Part 2. For an example see Edler, "White on White," 97.
7. Terry, *New Whites*, 3.

ambiguity of white privilege while fighting white privilege because that's real." And to Terry, racism wasn't just stereotyping either: "the elimination of stereotyping would go part of the way toward eliminating cultural racism, but it would not necessarily guarantee that cultural differences would be appreciated and affirmed." Stereotyping may not be equal to racism, but Terry's radical cultural relativism meant that it was racist to simply criticize potentially damaging cultural traits. Nor was racism merely discrimination to Terry either: "Institutional openness does not necessarily mean flexibility of standards and appreciation of difference." He criticized non-discrimination for being colorblind and actively advocated "color conscious" racial discrimination.[8]

By the close of 1970, the "Power + Prejudice" definition had entered into society, along with all the radical views that accompanied it. It implanted itself in what was likely people's first and only class on racism—teachers learned it from Delmo Della-Dora, industry workers and church-goers learned it from Robert Terry, and impressionable high school students learned it from Pat Bidol. It's not clear how successful Bidol's original curriculum was, nor Terry's corporate trainings; unlike Hurwitz and Snook's program, there are no course evaluations remaining in the available record. But Bidol was successful enough to be given the opportunity to revise her curriculum and spread it on the national level with the help of the NEA.[9] Other educators studying at the University of Massachusetts became enamored with her ideas—building curriculums that would have lasting influence even today.[10] And Terry was successful enough that the US military turned to his

---

8. Terry, *New Whites*, 3–6.

9. To be discussed Part 2. See National Education Association, *Education & Racism*.

10. Namely Judith Katz and James Edler, to be discussed in depth in Part 2. See Katz, *White Awareness*.

teachings to fight racism in the military in a massive failed experiment.[11]

---

11. To be discussed in Part 2. Also see Klein, "Far-left racism in government is nothing new."

Part Two

The Spread of "Power + Prejudice" & Racism Awareness Training

Pat Bidol Refines Her Curriculum and Trains Teachers

T he inception of "Power + Prejudice" was completed in 1970, but that inception is only half the story. How did these fringe white educators manage to spread their ideas so successfully that they even influenced a highly respected dictionary?[1]

As with Terry having his ideology of New White Consciousness accepted by major businesses, Anthony Downs convincing the United States Commission on Civil Rights to legitimize the black nationalist, Marxist ideology of Stokely Carmichael, and New

---

1. Part 2 serves as a follow-up to the origin of the "Power + Prejudice" definition and the creation of Racism Awareness Training. This section aims to cover the process of the spread of these ideas into the mainstream. While most of the core developments in the spread during the 1970s are described within, the bridge from the 1970s to the modern day has not been fully researched and described. Perceptive readers may have noticed the minimal impact from the field of Critical Theory in this story. Yet Critical Race Theory, and its subfield of Critical Whiteness Studies, are the most frequent target of blame for ideas similar and sometimes fully identical to Bidol and Terry's in the modern day. It would appear at some point that these schools of thought merged, perhaps with Critical Theory providing a post-hoc theoretical justification for ideas first developed by Bidol, Terry, Della-Dora, and others. The details of this remain a research project worthy of pursuit.

Detroit spreading the radicalism of rioters, the answer lies largely in the willingness of mainstream institutions to bring such ideas out of the fringe.

In 1972, Pat Bidol released a second edition of her curriculum. The second edition was published by "New Perspectives on Race (NPR)," a new subsidiary of New Detroit, Inc., which was co-directed by Bidol. It was using her curricula in both elementary and secondary school settings and developing materials for the preschool level.[2]

The second edition featured a significant change in prioritizing the "Power + Prejudice" definition, which was now more than a single bullet point. In this edition, it appears in the first paragraph of the first page, serving as a framework for the entire course:

> Racial tensions affect all levels of life in America. As documented by the Kerner, MOREL, Coleman, and Violence Commission reports, these tensions are

---

2. Co-director proof and details on NPR from New Perspectives on Race, "What Is New Perspectives on Race?"

Development for preschool level from New Perspectives on Race, "New Perspectives on Race," E-1/F-1.

In 1973 The Division of Minority Affairs of the Michigan Education Association published a "Multi Ethnic Handbook" targeted to 4th through 8th-grade classrooms, the youngest demographic in this historical period being taught these ideas with presently obtainable curriculum. The "Multi Ethnic Handbook" was a guidebook of lesson plans for teaching about racism and the contributions of minority groups. It included Delmo Della-Dora's definition of racism from "What Curriculum Leaders Can Do About Racism" that "racism is different from racial prejudice, hatred, or discrimination. Racism involves having the power to carry out systematic discriminatory practices through the major institutions of our society." It did not include any traditional dictionary definitions of racism. Under its definition of "white racism," it again quoted Della-Dora, writing, "racism and white racism mean the same thing ... When you combine power with racial discrimination, the result is racism." When differentiating individual racism from institutional racism, it quoted Stokely Carmichael's *Black Power*. Michigan Education Association, *Multi Ethnic Handbook*, 1: Later Elementary and Middle School, 0–7.

symptoms of the underlying white racism which
pervades our society. Racism is racial prejudice (the
belief that one's own race is superior to another race)
combined with the power to enforce this bias
throughout the institutions and culture of a society. In
our society white racial prejudices are reinforced by
our institutions and culture because we whites
presently control the decision making and standard-
setting processes within them. As a result, white-
originated standards are normative, which leads to
illegitimate privileges for whites, who are receiving
benefits just because they are white, and
subordination of blacks and other Third World
peoples, who are being oppressed because they are not
white.[3]

The second edition also assigned Robert Terry's essay "New
Whites—Justice and Racism."[4] Additionally, the influence of the
NTL Institute was explicit; NTL trainer Orian Warden, who had
extensive ties to Terry, was thanked in the acknowledgments of the
second edition. The revised curriculum also contained exercises for
students that were directly based on NTL materials, including one
that asked students to list the differences between the "behaviors of
whites" and the "behaviors of Third World Peoples."[5]

Notably, one change that made the revised curriculum even
more manipulative was its definition list for the word "prejudice."

---

3. Bidol, *Developing New Perspectives on Race*, Revised Edition, 1.
4. Bidol, *Developing New Perspectives on Race*, Revised Edition, 19.
5. Acknowledgment from Bidol, *Developing New Perspectives on Race*, Revised
Edition, iii.
   Exercise from Bidol, *Developing New Perspectives on Race*, Revised Edition, 12-
13.

Definitions for both "prejudice" and "racism" in the first edition came from the *Random House Dictionary of the English Language*, 1967. But the second edition replaced the definition of "prejudice" with that from *Webster's Seventh New Collegiate Dictionary*, 1967.

While Random House had as its first definition for prejudice an "unfavorable opinion or feeling formed beforehand without knowledge, thought or reason," the Webster's entry's first definition of prejudice was "injury or damage resulting from some judgment or action of another in disregard of one's rights." This definition allowed for the differentiation of "racism" from causing "injury or damage" based on racial judgment.[6]

Conveniently, Bidol did not update the second edition with Webster's definition of "racism," which would have undercut her framework. Webster's, like most other dictionaries at the time and today, defined racism as "a belief that race is the primary determinant of human traits and capacities and that racial differences produce an inherent superiority of a particular race" and, explicitly, "racial prejudice or discrimination."[7]

As Bidol was working for New Detroit, she was concurrently completing her doctorate in education (EdD) at the University of Michigan. In 1972, Bidol submitted her dissertation, "The Effects of Racism Awareness Training on the Professional Staff of an Education Association," studying the effectiveness of a 3-day "anti-racist" training for education professionals operated by NPR. Bidol explained why she believed her new approach to anti-racist trainings improved upon previous versions:

 Until the sixties most American behavioral scientists

---

6. Bidol, *Developing New Perspectives on Race*, Revised Edition, 19.
    Bidol, *Developing New Perspectives on Race*, 34.
7. *Webster's Seventh New Collegiate Dictionary*, 704.

were primarily concerned with the identification and elimination of racial prejudice. The resulting identified relationships between racial prejudice and mental illness resulted in a "sick personality approach." It was believed that if racially prejudiced individuals could be cured, racial prejudice would be eliminated. A psycho-dynamic explanation of racial prejudice includes those theses that hold that social prejudice originated in the infantile unconscious (Sterba, 1947); in "frustration-aggression" (Dollard, 1937); in a basic personality type (Adorno, 1950); and in the beliefs which form our very being (Kovel, 1970).

While there is indeed much validity in these studies, the overall result of focusing primarily on the psychology of the involved individuals is to distract our energies regarding possibilities for social structure change (Houser, 1965). If the involved individuals are cured of their racial prejudices; the institutional supports for racism are not necessarily altered. This approach, therefore, ignores the realities of systematic prejudice which operates at the personal, institutional, and cultural levels in American society. If racist beliefs and behaviors are viewed as being perpetuated by mentally ill individuals, the causes and manifestations of racism cannot be readily and rationally examined by all those who are involved (the victims, perpetuators, researchers). Logical societal-level solutions cannot be as readily identified (Thomas and Sillan, 1972).

If the problem of racial prejudice is identified as being more than just psychological, then both the social causes and psychological manifestations can be identified. Thus, the problem is one of "racial prejudice plus the power to enforce this bias throughout the institutions and culture of a society"; this is "racism" (Bidol, 1971). In reducing American racism attention must be given to all of the salient factors involved in the perpetuation of the oppression of peoples of color which results in the possession, whether desired or not, of illegitimate privileges for all who are white.[8]

If the primary goal is not ending racism as traditionally understood, but creating structural change that would remove all "illegitimate privileges" (following Carmichael's Marxism-Leninism, meaning any degree of inequality) in society, Bidol's redefinition serves that end by shifting the goalposts. When one participant in Bidol's training asked, "why isn't changing personal attitudes enough ... aren't institutions composed of individuals?" The training staff clarified that "we don't have time to eliminate the racism of each individual; institutions are influenced by the vested interests of those who are in control and making everyone feel better will not necessarily change the power relationships."[9]

However, in reality, it is individuals' psychological change that often causes social structures to change. For example, consider the witch trials that took place across pre-modern Europe and North America, famously including the Salem Witch Trials. Witch trials, like racism, resulted from widely held factually inaccurate and discriminatory views, which led to the deaths of 40,0000 to 60,000

---

8.   Bidol, "The Effects of Racism Awareness Training on the Staff of an Educational Association," 13-14.
9.   Bidol, "The Effects of Racism Awareness Training on the Staff of an Educational Association," 59.

people, mostly women who didn't fully conform to societal norms.[10] The Salem Witch Trials, which are widely considered one of America's most notorious cases of mass hysteria, eventually ended due to a greater societal understanding that witchcraft wasn't real. Theologians argued that witchcraft was mere superstition, and medical practitioners argued that witchcraft was a delusion. Witch trials began to disappear when enough individuals realized that they were based on wrong ideas. Likewise, to most Americans, if all individuals were cured of racial prejudice, under the traditional definition of racism, then racism would be considered over.

That has already occurred for many ethnic groups. For example, Italian Americans were stereotyped as more violent than the average American for much of history, despite the fact that Italian Americans had an arrest rate no greater than any other major immigrant group. Congress even passed legislation restricting immigration from Italy while exempting Northern European nations. Like African Americans, Italian Americans were lynched, treated with bias in criminal trials, and relegated to ethnic ghettos.[11] Although it is a myth that Italians were considered "black" in America, it is true that Italians, like Jews, were largely considered a separate race from America's Anglo-Saxon and Germanic majority.[12] Italians suffered from both prejudice and, as a predominantly poor immigrant class, a lack of power. Yet today, such racial distinctions are rarely made. Italian Americans, who suffered from prejudice and a lack of power, no longer suffer the damaging stereotypes and racialization that kept them oppressed. Over time, as more people began to realize that these ideas were false, they fell out

---

10. Hutton, "Writing the History of Witchcraft," 247.
11. Connell and Gardaphé, *Anti-Italianism.*
12. Bernstein, "Sorry, but the Irish were always 'white' (and so were Italians, Jews and so on)."

of fashion, and Italian Americans as a community have gone on to incredible success.

Yet the very first objective in Bidol's training program for education professionals was "to clearly distinguish racial prejudice from racism."[13] Its goal was also explicitly revolutionary in nature, despite the clear success of reducing individual racial prejudice as in the Italian American case. One trainer lectured participants that "it is more important to live for the revolution than to die for it."[14]

There was at least one genuine white racist who participated in the training, asking at one point "let's cut this bullshit. The real question A is—would you want to let your daughter marry a nigger."[15] Ironically, because Bidol's program was focused on the revolutionary redefinition of racism, not individual racial prejudice, it is unclear whether the training was able to have any influence on this participant's worldview.

Bidol's study of the results of her training aimed to find changes in her participant's "race ideology," defined in part as a "belief in the need for militant protests against racism" and "individual orientation" versus "system orientation." By "individual orientation," Bidol meant people attributing the status of their lives to their "internal control," and by "system orientation," she meant people attributing the status of their lives to "external control," such as "the white dominated and controlled institutions of our society." Bidol aimed to push the participants toward a system orientation, with the goal of inspiring them toward "the initiation of collective actions."[16]

---

13. Bidol, "The Effects of Racism Awareness Training on the Staff of an Educational Association," 32.

14. Bidol, "The Effects of Racism Awareness Training on the Staff of an Educational Association," 59.

15. Bidol, "The Effects of Racism Awareness Training on the Staff of an Educational Association," 59.

16. Bidol, "The Effects of Racism Awareness Training on the Staff of an Educational Association," 20.

Despite some conflict between groups of white participants, 80% of participants said their experience during the training was "positive." However, on a form handed out before the conference, only 3% of participants expected the training to be a negative experience, but on the post-conference survey, 11% of participants described their experience as negative.[17] While analysis of post-conference surveys showed only marginal change in participants' "race ideology," most of them "felt that they were now more aware of racism and that they were able to develop back-home action plans."[18]

Those "back-home action plans" were developed on the third and final day of the training. Fourteen participants created a project proposal regarding "racism awareness training for local school districts." Ten created a project proposal aiming to "make fellow whites move to anti-racist actions." Nine participants created a project proposal aimed at getting "racism awareness training included in teacher-training programs." Another project proposal sought "to establish an inservice human relations program [racism awareness training] for a large metropolitan school district" and was included in the teacher's union's bargaining package for their next

---

Low belief in self-efficacy can lead to a psychological state known as "learned helplessness," where since one believes that their effort cannot make a difference, they don't bother trying. That becomes a major hindrance when, in fact, making a difference in one's own life is possible. For more see Steel, "Self-Efficacy and Success: Is There Any Relationship?"

17. Bidol, "The Effects of Racism Awareness Training on the Staff of an Educational Association," 56.

In line with NTL's encounter group techniques, the staff desired "that the confrontations between the white participants should be increased." Attempts at physical intimidation occurred. Bidol, "The Effects of Racism Awareness Training on the Staff of an Educational Association," 61.

18. Race Ideology change from Bidol, "The Effects of Racism Awareness Training on the Staff of an Educational Association," 85-87

Quote from Bidol, "The Effects of Racism Awareness Training on the Staff of an Educational Association," 56.

negotiation. Assuming that all of these projects were completed, 33 additional Bidol-inspired training sessions or advocacy activities were sparked from this single three-day training.[19] Afterward, participants held a vote on whether the education association should provide additional Racism Awareness Training, which passed with a majority vote.[20]

NPR advertised its teacher trainings as seeking to create NTL-style change-agents:

> To provide a basic understanding of the processes of change, the focus will shift from an initial exploration of change theory to an individual/team design of back home change programs which will facilitate the removal of blocks to full participation of all members of their respective organization and institutions, and communities.[21]

Bidol's "change model" advocated "rebellion," defined as "[using] force to gain <u>control</u> of the situation and its resources," as well as "repression" of oppositional or challenging views and "co-option" of "the 'cause' of the challenging group as your own and advertis[ing] that you are better able to do something about it ... hitch the challenger's power or resources to your ends."[22] This is precisely what Bidol and those following her have done to the liberal and once dominant efforts to combat racism inspired by Martin Luther King.

---

19. Bidol, "The Effects of Racism Awareness Training on the Staff of an Educational Association," 70-71.
20. Bidol, "The Effects of Racism Awareness Training on the Staff of an Educational Association," 67.
21. New Perspectives on Race, "What Is New Perspectives on Race?"
22. Bidol, "The Effects of Racism Awareness Training on the Staff of an Educational Association," 139-140.

New Detroit staged "thousands" of race relations trainings through the end of 1973.[23] As of 1970, Jo-Ann Terry's New Detroit Speakers' Bureau received requests for an average of 160 speaking engagements each month, more than doubling the demand from 1969. New Detroit staff estimated that they had presented to over 315,000 individuals by the end of 1970.[24] Graduate school credits were offered at the University of Michigan, Michigan State University, Eastern Michigan University, and Wayne State University to students who completed NPR trainings.[25]

But these early efforts would pale in comparison to the influence that Bidol and NPR would soon have on a national audience of educators. Much of NPR's teacher trainings took place at MEA, an affiliate of the NEA.[26] Later, the NEA adopted Bidol's teacher trainings wholesale.

---

23. Burgin, "The Workshop as the Work," 140-141.
24. Burgin, "The Workshop as the Work," 141-142.
25. New Perspectives on Race, "New Perspectives on Race," G-1.
26. NPR trainings taking place at MEA from New Perspectives on Race, "What Is New Perspectives on Race?" and National Education Association, *Education & Racism*, 7.

MEA as an affiliate of NEA from Michigan Education Association, *About Us*.

NEA as the largest union from InfluenceWatch, "National Education Association (NEA)."

The NEA Spreads Racism
Awareness Training

I n the early 1970s, Bidol's views began to grow in popularity
outside of Michigan. The Illinois Education Association based
its curriculum on Bidol's, and NPR advised institutions such as the
US Navy and Air Force, the Young Women's Christian Association,
various community mental health organizations including the
California Institute of Mental Health, and numerous schools and
universities across the country.[1] Bidol's "Power + Prejudice"
definition even made it to the reaches of Harvard University, with
social psychology professor James M. Jones writing in his 1972 book
Prejudice and Racism that "racism defined as a set of beliefs or
attitudes represents little advance over the concept of race
prejudice. Consequently our definition of racism will go beyond
beliefs or attitudes to include actions ... Racism results from the

---

1. National Education Association, *Education & Racism,* 22.
    New Perspectives on Race, "New Perspectives on Race," B-1 to B-4.

transformation of race prejudice and/or ethnocentrism through the exercise of power against a racial group defined as inferior."[2]

The NEA was most influential in disseminating Bidol's views. In 1973, it published *Education & Racism: An Action Manual,* a workshop curriculum for teachers consisting of a three-day program in exactly the same model as Bidol described in her dissertation. Not attributed to any author, the curriculum was described as "the culmination of a year of cooperative effort between the Michigan Education Association's Human Relations Division and the Human Relations Section of NEA Teacher Rights ... working together, with invaluable assistance from New Perspectives on Race, Inc." The foreword also thanked "Dick Weber and Dr. Pat Bidol of New Perspectives on Race, Inc., ... for their assistance in planning the workshops and implementing the total program."[3] Amongst other radical literature, the bibliography cited the Black Panthers, Stokely Carmichael, and Robert Terry.[4]

The preface explained, "'if you are not part of the solution, you must be part of the problem.' White educators in the United States, to whom this report is addressed, are part of the problem." It described its purposes as "first, to provide a set of common understandings about racism and its origins and manifestations in our society. Second, to share two examples of how teacher organizations have successfully begun to deal with racism in educational settings (success being defined as having made a difference). Third, to suggest resources that will be useful to state and local associations in implementing antiracism programs."[5]

---

2. As with Bidol, why "racism" as a term needs or should be expected to advance anything beyond the concept of race prejudice remains unclear short of its political utility. Jones, *Prejudice and Racism,* 117.

3. National Education Association, *Education & Racism,* 7.

4. National Education Association, *Education & Racism,* 53-56.

5. National Education Association, *Education & Racism,* 8.

The NEA curriculum was nearly a replica of Bidol's previous curricula. Large portions of its introduction were lifted directly from Bidol's "Mini Lecture On Differences Between Prejudice and Racism," explaining that "if we are to work on the elimination of racism from our society it is advisable that we work from a commonly agreed-upon set of definitions ... In the United States at present, only whites can be racists ... blacks and other Third World peoples do not have access to the power to enforce any prejudices they may have, so they cannot, by definition, be racists. Racism equals prejudice plus power."[6] It also explained Robert Terry's idea that "when we profit knowingly or unknowingly from the past or present racism of other whites, we are racist," meaning the best white people can be are "antiracist/racists—those who recognize the illegitimate privileges obtained by whiteness but strive to remove these institutionally and culturally racist benefits even while receiving them."[7]

In the areas where the curriculum varied from Bidol's earlier versions, its content was often more direct and radical. For example, it viewed school systems' promotion of a balanced diet as cultural racism:

School systems reinforce white images and maintain the 'rightness of whiteness' syndrome through curriculum materials. In very subtle ways white aspirations, norms, and values are held out to [indecipherable word]. Look, for example at materials stressing the importance of eating three well balanced meals a day. The meals illustrated are white middle class meals, served as viewed appropriate by white

---

6. National Education Association, *Education & Racism,* 10, 12-13.
7. National Education Association, *Education & Racism,* 17-18.

standards and consisting of foods selected by whites as desirable. Black and Third World youngsters cannot identify with that image and can only regard their parents as failing them in some important way because they don't serve those same foods.[8]

Education & Racism's introduction also proposed that "only those who have been oppressed and repressed by whites can ascertain whether a proposed action will really help eliminate racism or merely allow it to continue in a new form."[9] This disregarded that the majority of black Americans disagreed with the ideas within the curriculum. New Detroit and Delmo Della-Dora's ignoring of dissenters was necessary for these ideas to develop and survive long enough to become an NEA curriculum. This NEA curriculum differed from other Racism Awareness Trainings in specifying that "these exercises, like all programs designed by whites to eradicate racism, should be implemented with the guidance of Third World people, who should be directly involved whenever possible ... all-white groups could actually reinforce the stereotypes they are attempting to identify, understand, and remove."[10]

The "heightened awareness" that training participants came away with had some negative effects. Some teachers struggled with "powerful feelings of anger at those who had taught them to be racist

---

8. National Education Association, *Education & Racism*, 15.
   The Michigan Education Association's "Multi Ethnic Handbook" also included this same idea, telling teachers that "the concept of the 'balanced meal' should be omitted because of the value-oriented implications." Michigan Education Association, *Multi Ethnic Handbook*, 1: Later Elementary and Middle School, 68.
9. National Education Association, *Education & Racism*, 19.
10. National Education Association, *Education & Racism*, 25.
   This would be a point of contention between activists who thought minorities must be a part of the process and activists who didn't want to burden minorities with the chore of fighting racism.

and at themselves for continuing old racist behaviors." One remarked, "how do I ever get comfortable with the knowledge that I am a racist?" At least one teacher believed that after participating in the training, he started treating black students worse; an observer detailed: "he had grown increasingly uncomfortable with his black students because he was so painfully aware of being part of the problem. 'I used to be colorblind, I thought, and now I cannot be. Am I more of a racist now?'" Participants identified the need for more racism awareness workshops in their own schools, and to find "ways to get access to power" and find "ways to approach peers and superiors so they aren't immediately turned off."[11]

Another new feature in the *Education & Racism* curricula was an "Assessment Checklist for White Racism." As examples of white racism, the checklist included statements such as "I should not be held responsible for the actions of my ancestors," "on the basis of statistics it's true that there is a higher crime rate in the ghetto," "I do not personally have responsibility for the policies of racist institutions," and "every person should be judged solely on his accomplishments, regardless of race." It also defined as racist the view that militants should not break the law. This checklist was developed by education graduate students at the University of Massachusetts. One of these graduate students, Jim Edler, along with fellow UMass student Judith Katz, would go on to have a major influence on the spread of Racism Awareness Training.[12]

---

11. National Education Association, *Education & Racism*, 32-39.
12. National Education Association, *Education & Racism*, 41-43.

The Military's Adoption of Racism Awareness Training

On July 20th, 1969, a battalion of Marines at Camp Lejeune, North Carolina had a party. Mid-way through the night, a white Marine entered and proclaimed that he had been assaulted by a group of black marines. Within thirty minutes, fifteen white Marines were attacked by black and Puerto Rican marines who yelled statements including "white beasts" and "call us niggers now." One white corporal died from his injuries; an investigation determined that neither he nor any of the other victims had participated in "any misconduct" or "any specific provocation."[1] This was the second time a white marine had been killed in a racial incident at Camp Lejeune; the prior killing occurred in November of 1968. Racism was commonplace in the camp and in the surrounding community, so the military, which considered itself "in

1. Burgin, "The Most Progressive and Forward Looking Race Relations Experiment in Existence," 1.

    House Committee on Armed Forces, *Inquiry into the Disturbances at Marine Corps Base.*

the vanguard of integration of the races," decided to make major structural changes.[2]

Two months later, in September 1969, the Army Chief of Staff Gen. William C. Westmoreland directed that race relations be incorporated into the Army's educational system, leading to a four-hour block of instruction at the Infantry School.[3] In 1970, Secretary of Defense Melvin Laird expanded this initiative and created the Inter-service Task Force on Education in Race Relations. In June of 1971, the Department of Defense issued Directive 1322.11, which established "An Education Program in Race Relations ... on a continuing basis for all military personnel," which prompted the founding of a Race Relations Education Board and the Defense Race Relations Institute (DRRI) to train full-time race relations instructors.[4] Between 1971 and 1974, every military employee was mandated to receive eighteen hours of race relations seminars. The vast majority of those seminar leaders were trained by DRRI. Over its first three years of operation, more than 2,500 service members were trained to teach race relations by DRRI.[5]

In light of the racial tensions at the time and the need for cohesiveness amongst service members, some form of training could

---

2. House Committee on Armed Forces, *Inquiry into the Disturbances at Marine Corps Base.*

3. Secretary of the Army's Senior Review Panel, *The Secretary of the Army's Senior Review Panel Report on Sexual Harassment,* 130.

Chief of Staff name from U.S. Army Center of Military History, "U.S. Army Chiefs of Staff."

4. Burgin, "The Most Progressive and Forward Looking Race Relations Experiment in Existence," 7.

Department of the Army, "No. 600-42 Race Relations Education for the Army," 1.

Defense Equal Opportunity Management Institute, "About DEOMI."

Department of Defense, "No. 1322.11 Department of Defense Education in Race Relations for Armed Forces Personnel."

5. Burgin, "The Most Progressive and Forward Looking Race Relations Experiment in Existence," 7.

have been beneficial. Within the Army, only 58% of whites and 23% of blacks felt "blacks are treated exactly the same as whites in the Army."[6] Army regulations explained that the objective of race relations education was "to maintain the highest degree of organizational and combat readiness by fostering harmonious relations among all military personnel under army control." Those same regulations explicitly defined the traditional "personal (individual) racism" as "the acting out of prejudices by individuals against other individuals or groups along racial lines," and its definition of institutional racism—"the policies or actions of an institution which have racially differential effects not otherwise justifiable"—was more reasonable than Carmichael's because of its inclusion of the phrase "otherwise justifiable."[7] But in practice, this was not what was taught to participating service members.

Military leaders asserted that "black militancy" caused the violence at Camp Lejeune, and that it could be stemmed through education by DRRI. Yet from 1970 to 1974, rather than treating militancy as a problem to be solved, DRRI taught the militant-inspired views that had come out of New Detroit.[8]

NPR consulted with DRRI, and Terry's *For Whites Only* "proved crucial" to DRRI's work.[9] According to Critical Whiteness Studies scholar Say Burgin:

 Terry's book pointedly pitched these ideas to whites,

---

6.   Army Infantry School, *Race Relations Orientation Packet for Leaders*, 9.

7.   Army Infantry School, *Race Relations Orientation Packet for Leaders*, 1.

8.   Burgin, "The Most Progressive and Forward Looking Race Relations Experiment in Existence," 2.

Black militancy as at fault from House Committee on Armed Forces, *Inquiry into the Disturbances at Marine Corps Base*.

9.   New Perspectives on Race, "New Perspectives on Race," B-4.

Burgin, "The Most Progressive and Forward Looking Race Relations Experiment in Existence," 9.

and, I would suggest, it allowed the Institute to espouse Black Power ideals in the early 70s without having to use the work of more controversial figures like Carmichael and Cleaver, though they clearly impacted Terry's ideas. Terry's book, then, provided a back door into Black Power for DRRI. Whereas color-blindness had begun to dominate mainstream discussion of racism in the US, DRRI's ideology in the early 1970s remained more closely aligned with the Black Power turn.

The emphasis on whiteness as problematic was central in this, and here, DRRI's reliance on Terry was great.[10]

DRRI used *For Whites Only* as reading material in its programs and taught, as Terry did, "that whites in the military had to develop a new consciousness in order to combat racism. It maintained that racism was a problem created and sustained by whites and white-dominated institutions ... Cultural racism also ensured that they could not escape a racially prejudiced upbringing." And DRRI materials expressed that "whites, thus, had both the power and the prejudice necessary to maintain racist systems." DRRI's primary goal was achieving "recognition from whites that they must 'accept responsibility' for racism in the military." DRRI's goal thus explicitly contradicted the military's prior analysis, which had prompted the very founding of DRRI, which was that the 1969 murder at Camp Lejeune was caused by black militancy which "fanned the flames" without "any specific provocation" from white personnel.[11]

---

10. Burgin, "The Most Progressive and Forward Looking Race Relations Experiment in Existence," 10.
11. Burgin, "The Most Progressive and Forward Looking Race Relations Experiment in Existence," 10-11.

Students at DRRI were mostly volunteers, though many were sent by commanders who wanted to get rid of their underperforming service members. The training was an intensive seven weeks of constant engagement with seminar facilitators and other inductees while living on the base. It was also, as one might expect, filled with conflict; discussion group confrontation led to the "isolation" of students while they were expected to consider the "impact" of their prejudices. Students were put into two-person teams of one officer and one enlisted person, of whom one was white and one was non-white. Those teams generally stayed together after leaving DRRI, co-leading race relations seminars at bases across the world.[12]

Each branch of the military integrated DRRI's efforts differently. The Army appeared particularly enthused, opening a race relations school in Oberammergau, Germany to supplement the work of DRRI graduates.[13] Under Army Regulation 600-21, the first four weeks of basic training included a mandatory race relations course for all soldiers of every unit.[14] For officers the training was more extensive, and a guidebook developed for officers taught as Bidol did that:

> no individual can be racist in isolation. He must be able to translate his racial prejudice into societal forms that perpetuate a particular color group's advantages over another color group. ... Although blacks in our society can be prejudiced—misjudge a particular

---

Camp Lejeune analysis from House Committee on Armed Forces, *Inquiry into the Disturbances at Marine Corps Base.*

12. Burgin, "The Most Progressive and Forward Looking Race Relations Experiment in Existence," 8.

13. Burgin, "The Most Progressive and Forward Looking Race Relations Experiment in Existence," 11.

14. Thomas and Nordlie, *Race Relations and Equal Opportunity in the Army*, 83.
    Army Infantry School, *Race Relations Orientation Packet for Leaders*, 22.

situation because of scanty data—blacks cannot be racist in America regardless of their views— prejudiced or not. They are not in a sufficiently influential stance as yet to translate, unilaterally their objectives into power, structure and cultural form.

The guidebook laid out in detail its case for why racial discrimination and racism were not the same, which explicitly contradicted the "equal opportunity" policy of the Department of Defense at the time:

There are two limitations to the concept of discrimination and its counterpart non-discrimination which keep it from being identical with racism and the elimination of racism. The conceptual problems can be most clearly illustrated by returning to the opening example of creating a racist community. Non-discrimination policies usually overlook the group phenomenon. Rather, they focus on blacks [sic] to individual inclusion ("let a few blacks in but don't threaten the power"). Furthermore non-discrimination policies usually assume the predominant cultural standards as given. Institutional openness does not necessarily mean flexibility of standards and appreciation of difference. So, in practice, open housing has meant in America letting individual blacks and other color groups into white communities on white terms. A non-discriminatory stance usually does not encourage powerful groups of blacks to move in nor does it mobilize whites to question their own cultural standards and seek alternatives.

There is a second problem with the notions of

discrimination and non-discrimination. Racial discrimination is color conscious, non-discrimination is color blind. During the non-discriminatory phase of government intervention in industrial hiring for example, all records of color were to be stricken from applications and promotion files. "If color is a block, eliminate the color criteria" the argument went. However, even if color codes were eliminated (too many cases prove whites found other devious ways to track blacks), the non-discriminatory posture did not increase dramatically the flow of minorities into key positions in corporations and unions nor did it accelerate minority migration into white communities. Non-discriminatory policies stressed individual inclusion and kept the group power clearly white; informal and formal standards created an alien atmosphere which forces blacks to assume white styles in order to make it in the organization. What anti-racists have learned is that color blind anti-exclusion policies don't work. What are needed are color conscious aggressive inclusion to guarantee equal employment opportunity. ... anti-discrimination is not a full-blown anti-racist approach because of limited attention to group power and ethnocentric standards. Most, if not all, anti-discrimination programs ignore the need for a total new white consciousness.[15]

That argument, explicitly mentioning Terry's "new white consciousness," cited a publication from the Detroit Industrial

---

15. Army Infantry School, *Race Relations Orientation Packet for Leaders*, 154.

Mission.[16] Officers were told that "the roots of prejudice run deep in most American lives. Feeling guilty about this is not helpful. You cannot change the fact that you were educated in this prejudicial fashion. However, you can change your behavior and that of your subordinates when you become aware that you do have prejudices which are discriminatory." No space was left for the possibility that a white person might not be prejudiced. Although the army's materials did not say so outright, they implied that the best a white person could be was an anti-racist racist, as all white Americans were prejudiced, all had power, and racism was defined as "Power + Prejudice." Officers were given a reading list that included Terry's *For Whites Only*, along with books from Eldridge Cleaver, Malcolm X, and the Kerner Commission Report, and were told that reading them were "some of the most progressive actions you as a commander can do."[17]

For officers teaching these ideas, the guidebook advised leaders on how to handle issues that regularly arose, such as that "groups may tend to be irrational (distort facts) ... in order to avoid the job at hand." When such disagreement with the material occurred, leaders were advised to focus on the disagreement, restate the purpose of the meeting, and consider if their own poor communication of the ideas was the cause of the negative response.[18] Any legitimate cause for disagreement was dismissed on the grounds that "troops often times will respond unreasonably to authority because of their own previous conflicts with the authority of their parents."[19]

Commanders regularly criticized these trainings, along with the army's contemporaneous so-called "equal opportunity" affirmative action policies, for "weakening the chain of command, decreasing

16. Army Infantry School, *Race Relations Orientation Packet for Leaders*, 156.
17. Army Infantry School, *Race Relations Orientation Packet for Leaders*, 172.
18. Army Infantry School, *Race Relations Orientation Packet for Leaders*, 6.
19. Army Infantry School, *Race Relations Orientation Packet for Leaders*, 4.

mission effectiveness, and lowering standards in general." At least one commander complained that "EOT [Equal Opportunity Treatment] programs are <u>causing</u> race problems—the more you talk about racial differences and the more you put emphasis on them, the more trouble you're going to have. Putting emphasis on the problem just exacerbates it."[20] While this point of view was reported to race relations leaders, the critique did not appear to be taken seriously by those designing the program, who instead advocated for expanding race relations training to the children and wives of service members.[21]

In addition to helping lead trainings, officers were advised that since "vocal militants... have considerable influence over peers, if for no other reason than their vehemence and audacity" that "for an effective race relations program, these men should be brought into the formal power structure." It was argued that "properly applied, this policy for using militants and emergent leader should: ... help combat extremist views on racial issues; and encourage the controlled use of radical or militant enthusiasm."[22]

Ultimately, DRRI's radical curriculum would not last. Commanders accused DRRI of brainwashing soldiers and creating "race militants" who were "subvert[ing] the normal activities of the military." The Pentagon launched an investigation into DRRI and concluded that it was "overzealous in its initial training methods" and asked that it "modify its approach so that individuals leaving the institute would not appear too militant." Additionally, the House Armed Services Committee reported that race relations trainings might have weakened military discipline, closed all branch-specific race relations schools, and dropped 700 race relations instructors

---

20. Army Infantry School, *Race Relations Orientation Packet for Leaders*, 10.
21. Army Infantry School, *Race Relations Orientation Packet for Leaders*, 18.
22. Army Infantry School, *Race Relations Orientation Packet for Leaders*, 192.

and managers from the budget.[23] After 1974, the trainings changed in order. According to Richard Hope, who worked at DRRI:

 The content of the curriculum changed from a black/white confrontation to one increasingly less direct and more academic in direction...DRRI was ultimately to develop a more conservative approach to the study and training of race relations instructors. In the future, discussions were to stress ways of improving military intergroup relations and to devote less time to examining racism in military history.

70 percent of DRRI's graduates before 1974 worked full time teaching race relations, but by 1976 that had dropped to only 10 percent.[24]

While the decline of race relations training in the military may have been a victory for those opposed to the views of Carmichael, Terry, and Bidol, it was also a lost opportunity to fight the genuine racism that did exist in the military; the race relations issues at Camp Lejeune and elsewhere that initially led the Department of Defense to found DRRI were real and substantial. The story of what DRRI taught is also the story of what was not taught: the mainstream anti-racist ideology of Martin Luther King, Jr. Far too many service members of the time were not colorblind humanists, but it might have been a better world for service members of all races had they been trained to be.

DRRI still exists today under a new name, the Defense Equal Opportunity Management Institute (DEOMI). DEOMI was the

---

23. Burgin, "The Most Progressive and Forward Looking Race Relations Experiment in Existence," 14.
24. Burgin, "The Most Progressive and Forward Looking Race Relations Experiment in Existence," 15.

focus of controversy in 2015 when a journalist uncovered their training materials which taught that the Constitution and the Declaration of Independence have "historical influence that allows sexism to continue," and again in 2020 when the conservative group Judicial Watch, through a Freedom of Information Act request, received DEOMI documents that revealed they were teaching that it is bad to agree that "human similarities are more important than differences" and that an example of "modern racism" is believing that the "tactics and demands of activists are unfair."[25]

The 2020 release of DEOMI documents revealed, however, that they were now teaching that "prejudice and discrimination based on differences" is the primary definition of "racism."[26]

25. Goldenberg, "Defense Department: The Bible, Constitution and Declaration of Independence All Perpetuate Sexism."

Judicial Watch, "Judicial Watch Obtains Pentagon Anti-Bias Training Materials."

26. Defense Equal Opportunity Management Institute, *Defense Equal Opp Mgt FOIA*, 155.

People Acting for Change Together

B y the Summer of 1974, DIM had succeeded in getting many of the city's major companies as clients, including National Cash Register, Proctor & Gamble, Bundy, Dayton-Hudson, Detroit Edison, Sanders, and Borg-Warner.[1] But Jo-Ann Terry's New Detroit Speakers Bureau had an even greater reach in the Detroit area, organizing thousands of free race relations events. By the summer of 1971, the Speakers Bureau had adopted Bidol's definition of racism as one of their three major areas of focus:[2]

> 1. New black consciousness, including an awareness and understanding of black history and the new mood in the country's contemporary black community in its struggle for liberation from racism.
> 2. White racism, stressing individual, institutional

---

1. Burgin, "The Workshop as the Work," 76.
2. Thousands number from Burgin, "The Workshop as the Work," 140.

and cultural aspects (and understanding its difference from prejudice and discrimination.)

3. A new white consciousness, which proposes the development of a new identity for whites which seeks to unite the fight against racism with a new positive affirmation of whiteness.[3]

By 1972, the Speakers' Bureau changed its name to People Acting for Change Together (PACT), reflecting their self-perception as "change agents" in line with the philosophy of NTL.[4] PACT shared its office building with the Michigan Advisory Committee to the US Commission on Civil Rights, of which Jo-Ann Terry was also the chairperson. PACT was also expanding at that time, with the Center for Resources on Institutional Oppression (CRIO) spinning off from PACT. CRIO's main goal was to "facilitate the development of an active, national network of communication that links together groups and individuals who are combatting racism and related forms of institutional oppression." CRIO was directed by David J. Snider and also shared the same office building as PACT.[5]

---

3. Burgin, "The Workshop as the Work," 136.

4. Burgin, "The Workshop as the Work," 142.

5. PACT Office address from Bryant, Huber, and Stowe, *Resources for School Change*, 70.

Michigan Advisory Committee to the US Commission on Civil Rights address and Jo-Ann Terry as chairperson from Michigan Advisory Committee to the U.S. Commission on Civil Rights, "Civil Rights and the Housing and Community Development Act of 1974."

CRIO address and description from Center for Resources on Institutional Oppression to Joint Strategy and Action Committee, "A Proposal from the Center for Resources on Institutional Oppression," 2-3.

Building photo from City of Detroit Historic Designation Advisory Board, "Madison Office Building."

The historic building housing PACT's offices at 163 Madison St., Detroit.

Starting that summer, in 1972, PACT was presented with a major opportunity to reach children when they were asked by the Detroit Youth Board to train summer camp staff throughout the city. This would lead PACT volunteers to create another spinoff organization, the Community Committee for Alternative Camping, which aimed to "build a living situation where ethnic/racial differences were appreciated, not sublimated."[6] PACT also ran multi-week training sessions in churches and synagogues during this time, covering subjects like "what does it mean to be white?"[7]

Despite their ostensible success in securing training contracts, PACT's content often did not resonate with attendees. One participant wrote to Max Fisher, then-head of New Detroit, complaining that "a number of people, black and white ... used the [training] to give vent to their own hates, prejudices and general

6. Burgin, "The Workshop as the Work," 144-145.
7. Burgin, "The Workshop as the Work," 147-148.

nihilist philosophies', ... to unbelievably vitriolic anti-white, anti-semitic [sic], obscene diatribes."[8]

Seven years removed from the riot that led to its creation, recognizing that in New Detroit's early days "anything that could be sold as being new or innovative stood a good chance of being funded, if it was presented forcefully enough or by the right person," in 1974, New Detroit defunded both Bidol's NPR and PACT. New Detroit had come to the realization that "the conceptual framework of most of these groups is poor," and decided that "anti-racism efforts" should no longer be their priority.[9] Wayne County Community College would house a smaller PACT for the remainder of the decade.[10] Even in its limited state, PACT would diligently continue its efforts, even putting on summer camps of its own. One attendee of their 1976 camp recalled that they included many "awareness-raising exercises" and that she "learn[ed] a lot about being white."[11]

As Detroit began to recede from its position as the mecca of Racism Awareness Training, the anti-racism ideologies that were conceived in Detroit began to take off elsewhere. In February of 1972, NPR ran a Racism Awareness Training at the University of Massachusetts (UMass) graduate school of education.[12] It appears to have had a profound impact on their students.

---

8. Burgin, "The Workshop as the Work," 138.
    "[sic]" appears in Burgin's quote of the original material.
9. Burgin, "The Workshop as the Work," 154.
    Quotes from Colding, "Memo To: Lawrence P. Doss & Walter Douglass."
10. Burgin, "The Workshop as the Work," 157.
11. Nielsen, "The Heat Is On."
12. New Perspectives on Race, "New Perspectives on Race," B-2.

James Edler and the Mental Illness of Dissent

In 1974, James "Jim" Merryweather Edler submitted his EdD dissertation at UMass, "White on White: An Anti-Racism Manual for White Educators in the Process of Becoming." Like Terry, whom he cites extensively, Edler's dissertation aimed to provide a framework for the levels of white awareness, which he described as a journey progressing from "No Racial Problems Perceived," through "Existence of the Black Problem," "The White Liberal," and "Existence of the White Problem," finally culminating in "The New White Anti-Racist."[1]

Edler lamented that "so few other white Americans are cognizant of white affliction."[2] This "white affliction," he claims, is a "psychologically sophisticated blindness" in which "white Americans are unable or unwilling to see clearly the psychological or physical sufferings that permeate the lives of most Third World* people and how it is maintained, intentionally and unintentionally,

---

1. Edler, "White on White," viii.
2. Edler, "White on White," 1.

by white people."[3] According to Edler, before the advent of the "new white," white people had gone through "several hundred years of misperceiving reality." Correcting this misperception is no easy task; Edler explains that to get out of white people's "brainwashing," "escape means breaking away from the myths and the lies that have distorted our views about whiteness ... A true escape involves a thorough re-education about the meaning and intensity of the entrapment and a concerted effort to stay close enough to facilitate the re-education of other white Americans so they may comprehend their imprisonment."[4] Edler favorably cites Bidol, regurgitating her view that the best a white person can be is an "anti-racist racist," and expanding on it with his belief "that it is impossible for a white American to interact with a Black person and not have color be a conscious or unconscious issue."[5] To reach "The New White Anti-Racist" stage in their development, white people must get to the point where they can see the "true racial sickness of whites."[6] Edler was not speaking metaphorically: he literally believed that all white people suffered from "the mental illness of seeing reality inaccurately."[7] Edler seemed not to mind that his beliefs would be considered straightforwardly racist by the traditional definition of the term. When a critic accused him of "generaliz[ing] about [the] behavior" of certain racial groups, he dismissed the concern as "liberal jargon."[8]

Edler's "White on White" EdD dissertation was odd in that it

---

3. Edler, "White on White," 2.

In a footnote on this page marked with the "*," Edler clarified by "Third Word people" he meant "people of color." He used this term in part because he believed "'non-white' is a racist term implying that whiteness is the acceptable norm."

4. Edler, "White on White," 61.
5. Edler, "White on White," 89 and 99.
6. Edler, "White on White," 77.
7. Edler, "White on White," 96.
8. Edler, "White on White," 122.

featured little study or analysis of the field of education. Instead, Edler spends the bulk of it describing his story of how he arrived at his "new white" perspective and encouraging others to embark on the journey as well. One part that stands out about his story is how he was deeply influenced by an interracial encounter group he participated in during a training at the NTL Institute.

Edler saw himself as a white liberal before his time at NTL, where he experienced what he describes as an "awakening." In language resembling someone who has attained spiritual enlightenment, Edler said that the NTL training made him feel "far more energetic and free," and that the experience led to an upheaval of every aspect of his worldview.[9] He felt that he had changed so fundamentally that he was scared about how his own wife would see him when he returned.[10]

Like Terry acknowledged before him, "new whites" could face substantial issues integrating into mainstream society. Edler recognized the problem of "loneliness," remarking that "new whites must come to terms with being ostrasized [sic]." He would often initiate that ostracization himself by "cut[ing] relationships off" when people were "neive [sic] about their racism." The psychological impact of Edler's awakening was debilitating; Edler recalled repeating many times in conversation, "I'm tired of being angry at everyone. I'm burned out! The mistrust and disappointment take so much out of me." He recalled that "every place I go, I end up being upset; upset at television, the news broadcasts, at the newspaper, at jokes, at teachers, and even at friends."[11] Yet despite these maleffects, as faith would guide one to do, he felt so certain in his new understanding of the truth that

---

9. Edler, "White on White," 95.
10. Edler, "White on White," 92.
11. Edler, "White on White," 102-103.

"waiting until I knew what to do or had all the facts seemed like …
avoidance behavior."[12]

That concept of "avoidance" represents Edler's greatest
contribution to the development of Racism Awareness Training:

> Another helpful issue to discuss with individuals is
> the concept of distancing behaviors. These are
> behaviors that white people use to keep a physical and
> psychological distance between themselves and their
> potential implication in the white problem.* My
> realization of the existence of this category of
> behaviors occurred when a friend and I attended a
> scheduled presentation that was to deal with racism in
> America. The large room filled with white students
> and faculty but no one arrived to present the program.
> Nervous chatter increased as the room full of people
> had waited close to a half hour without the arrival of
> the guest presenter. A number of people began
> leaving but many remained for reasons that are
> unclear. My friend and I stayed and observed the
> white group go through a number of behaviors that I
> eventually labeled as "Distancing Behaviors." After
> observing individuals and small groups within the
> room, presumably sophisticated in their need to look
> at and act on our white problem, I identified about ten
> basic distancing behaviors. The reaction from most
> was silence but a few disagreed with my observations

12. Edler, "White on White," 92.
    The parallels between Edler's experience and that of religious experience ought
to be clear. While this author remains agnostic on whether "wokeness" ought to be
formally classified as a religion, Professor John McWhorter has compellingly argued
that it should be. For more see McWhorter, *Woke Racism*.

and most everyone left the room. Never before had I seen so clearly how we white Americans protect ourselves by Intellectualizing or game-playing of some kind. The experience prompted by the support of a friend, generated my development of the article cited in Appendix B.[13]

Appendix B was another work of Edler's, an essay titled "Distancing Behaviors Among White Groups Dealing With Racism." Here, in line with his position that whites were mentally ill for not holding his views, Edler essentially argued that any method of disagreeing with his "new white" position was inherently illegitimate.

The first of these distancing behaviors was "The 'Definition Game,'" a direct example of hypocrisy and double standards:

A common strategy in most white groups is to request a clear, concise definition of the word "racism." This can lead to hours and even weeks of debate while everyone defines the term with various jargon and favorite social science phrases. It is almost impossible to disagree with the need for a definition of terms but why do these "definers" spend so little time with a dictionary when discussing religion, politics, morals, or capitalism? The usual result is that the term is not publically [sic] defined other than what folks understood the word to connote hours earlier. This game is not to be confused with the actual need to

---

13. Edler, "White on White," 119.
    The "*" also directed readers to Appendix B.

clarify why the group is meeting or the differences between racism, discrimination and prejudice.[14]

Another was "The 'Distinguished Lecturer' Game," where Edler criticized any sharing of expert opinions that did not mirror his own:

 This game can be easily identified by the intense intellectualization and academic treatment of everyone's comments. The person with some background in recent publications can easily dominate this endeavor. We all play this game at various times when we "deal" with a problem by talking about it. Experts abound on the topic of racism but there seems to be little action in our community of white theorists. The cause is often a product of their distorted focus on the wrong problem—that is a denial of the white problem and an emphasis on blaming the victims for their situation. This lecture game, as with many others, puts a "gardol shield" between us and other members in the group with which we are involved because they often wish not to reveal less intellectual prowess. One of the sickest manifestations of this game is when whites become experts on what it's like to be Black. Many of us have heard white groups spend hours talking about Blacks and "their" problem. Although far more threatening and difficult,

---

14. Edler, "White on White," 186.

Edler specifically directed readers to Bidol, *Developing New Perspectives on Race*, Revised Edition, for how to clarify the differences between those words. Edler, "White on White," 160.

it is imperative that we look at "our" problem and our potential as change agents within white America![15]

That issue of whites expressing expertise on what it's like to be black, something inherent in Edler's own practices, might have been easily avoided were it not for "The 'Where are the Blacks?' Game":

Our ignorance of racism is exemplified many times as we demand that we need members of minority groups present for us to understand ourselves. This game often springs from the Definition Game and reveals a prevailing myth in the white community; namely that to deal with racism cannot be accomplished among an all-white group. After 350 years of being told there is a racial problem in this country, we begin our awakening but seem to still need confirmation. How many of us have genuinely dealt with the question of crime or politics, for example, without the presence of a criminal or politician? The real hypocrisy entails the white person's expectation of minority members to come running when the time to go to work is determined by the oppressor. It is vital that we understand such attitudes as distressingly racist and self-defeating from their onset. A friend once painted the analogy of a white man holding a Black man down with his foot on the Black man's neck while asking the man on the floor, "What can I do?"[16]

15. Edler, "White on White," 188.
16. Edler, "White on White," 187.

"The 'Instant Solution' Game" rejected solutions to racism other than Edler's simply for being too easy:

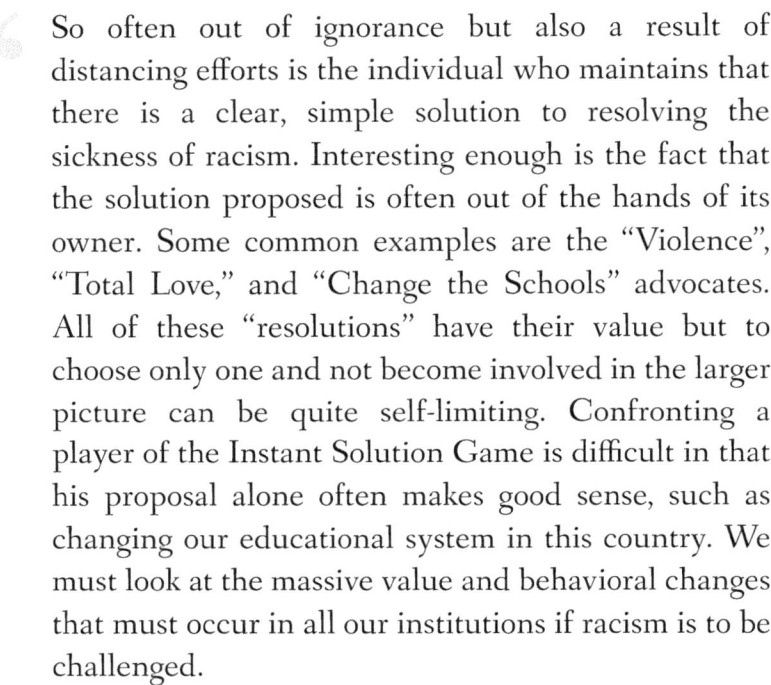

> So often out of ignorance but also a result of distancing efforts is the individual who maintains that there is a clear, simple solution to resolving the sickness of racism. Interesting enough is the fact that the solution proposed is often out of the hands of its owner. Some common examples are the "Violence", "Total Love," and "Change the Schools" advocates. All of these "resolutions" have their value but to choose only one and not become involved in the larger picture can be quite self-limiting. Confronting a player of the Instant Solution Game is difficult in that his proposal alone often makes good sense, such as changing our educational system in this country. We must look at the massive value and behavioral changes that must occur in all our institutions if racism is to be challenged.
>
> Such an effort is closely related to the technique of talking about racism from a frame of reference of "how things should be" rather than how they are. These gamesters insist that others should simply "treat everyone as an equal like I do." It would be nice if such equality were a reality, but the blatant injustices around us in this day and year make such suggestions an oversimplified and ineffective response.[17]

Why getting others to "treat everyone as an equal" would be

---

17. Edler, "White on White," 189.

harder than getting all whites to accept Edler's "new white" positions was left unelaborated upon.

And acknowledging data contrary to the notion that racism was a problem of the type and scale that Edler believed was just another distancing behavior too, "The 'You've Come a Long Way, Baby' Game":

> The last distancing behavior to be identified ends up being a rationale for personally slowing down or even completely avoiding the responsibilities for confronting racism. This game player emphasizes the "great strides that have been made in recent years." He may even complain that the Chicanos in his town are getting summer jobs before the whites! After hundreds of years of degradation, it must be amusing to hear the white man complain because he isn't getting as much preferential treatment as he once "enjoyed." Another segment of this behavior involves withdrawing into the adage of "it takes time—you can't change the world overnight." Use care to avoid playing this game because of its inherent alienating effect on others who actually understand racism today.[18]

Edler also included an "Inventory of Distancing Reactions to White Implications in Racism." It consisted of fifty "reactions" formatted in bullet points, including "racism doesn't affect my area of interest. (e.g. math)," "I'm not racist," and "I treat people as individuals no matter what color they are." Some of them seemed to be reactions that Edler would presumably support but found insufficient, such as "oh, yes, it's a terrible problem. But I'm doing

---

18. Edler, "White on White," 192-193.

something about it. I contribute money to the Black College Fund,"
"I'm doing all I can," and "I'm scared! I don't know what to do! Tell
me what to do!"[19]

Edler's paper on distancing behaviors was frequently cited by
his contemporaries. By pathologizing his intellectual critics as
"distancing" themselves from the preordained truth, its effect
appears to have been closing the door to any possibility for dialogue
with their critics.[20] One of his classmates at UMass, Judith Katz,
would take Edler's theory of "distancing" and weave it into Bidol's
anti-racist teaching philosophy.

---

19. Edler, "White on White," 194-197.

20. It is noteworthy, however, that Edler would have disagreed with certain ways in
which "anti-racism" is manifesting today. Edler wrote, "there are several unfortunate
motivations that have been the cause for white people joining an often chic anti-racist
group. These include: (1) Guilt Abolition, where an individual is motivated by a
sense of guilt rather than an understanding of racism; (2) Getting Even, where the
individual uses the activism to hurt or disappoint someone like a parent or spouse; (3)
Avoidance of Responsibilities, where the activist may be denying or avoiding other
expectations or responsibilities while using the importance of the racism issue as a
justification for avoidance; and (4) Forced Participation, where an individual has little
or no choice of involvement. Here the standard reaction becomes a repulsion of the
issue that appears to be forcing their involvement." Edler, "White on White," 134.

Judith Katz Popularizes Racism Awareness Training

In October of 1975, Judith Helen Katz submitted her EdD dissertation, "A Systematic Handbook of Exercises For The Re-Education of White People With Respect To Racist Attitudes And Behaviors," which three years later was reorganized and revised for her first book, *White Awareness: Handbook for Anti-Racism Training.*[1]

Katz's training sought to take white participants through six stages:

 Stage 1 lays the groundwork for participants to understand racism in society and in themselves. In this first stage the key concepts prejudice and racism are explored. The participants become aware of the

---

1. A revised edition would be published as recently as 2003. Katz, *White Awareness*, 2003.

reality that power is the major factor differentiating racism and prejudice.[2]

Stage 2 probes institutional racism. Participants are further confronted with the discrepancies in American ideology and behavior.

Stage 3 is designed to help participants sort through some of the feelings and reactions that were triggered in the previous stages. Feelings of fear, projection and guilt are brought to the surface.

Stage 4 explores cultural racism, including an examination of language, music, norms, and values. Attention is focused on White ethnocentrism and cultural differences.

Stage 5 centers around the meaning of whiteness and helps participants claim their White identity as an essential part of themselves. In this stage participants explore their own prejudices and personal roles in supporting racism.

Stage 6 helps participants develop specific action strategies to combat personal and institutional racism

---

2. That Katz grounded the participants' development in this understanding ought alone to demonstrate the massive degree of her reliance on Bidol, but this section also directly copied exercises previously developed by Bidol and used in "Developing New Perspectives on Race." Katz was even more explicitly manipulative than Bidol however. Where Bidol's exercise simply laid out definitions for "prejudice" and "racism" and used them as the basis for discussion, Katz's didn't just read between the lines, actively instructing the facilitator that, "it is important to push for the understanding that racism is prejudice plus power and that, therefore, Third World people cannot be racist against Whites in the United States. Third World people can be prejudiced against Whites, but clearly they do not have the power to enforce that prejudice. Although participants may not at this point totally accept this view or feel comfortable with it, it is important to establish the concept as a working definition. As the course progresses, it will, it is hoped, be better understood by participants." Katz, *White Awareness*, 1978, 50.

and define their next steps in becoming anti-racist (Katz and Ivey, 1977).[3]

Katz borrows much from Bidol's work. She not only draws influence from Bidol's "Developing New Perspectives on Race," but appropriates whole exercises, as well as Bidol's "Racism Definition List." Katz also asked training facilitators to use Bidol's "Mini-Lecture on the Difference Between Prejudice and Racism."[4]

Katz cited and assigned readings from Terry as well, including *For Whites Only* and "New Whites—Justice and Racism."[5] Her classmate James Edler's work was integrated repeatedly, including his "Distancing Behaviors" essay.[6] She wrote about NTL-style T-Groups, recommending that they be used in every session for at least one exercise (Katz would go on to become a board member at NTL).[7] Katz also cited Carmichael & Hamilton's *Black Power*, the Kerner Commission, Frank Joyce, Jones' *Prejudice & Racism*, and other materials from PACT.[8] Katz drew so much on these earlier theories that her work could be thought of as a synthesis of them all, adding only minor alterations.

However, other investigations into the history of Racism Awareness Training have identified the publications of Katz's *White Awareness* as the key event that precipitated these trainings taking off in popularity.[9] Google Scholar would appear to lend credence to

---

3. Katz, *White Awareness*, 1978, 26.
4. Katz, *White Awareness*, 1978, 41, 58, and 142.
5. Katz, *White Awareness*, 1978, 186, and 196.
6. Katz, *White Awareness*, 1978, 195.
7. Katz, *White Awareness*, 1978, 16-17 and 96.
   Katz as board member from Kaleel Jamison Consulting Group, Inc., "Judith H. Katz."
8. Katz, *White Awareness*, 1978, 201-205.
9. See Sivanandan, "RAT and the Degradation of Black Struggle" and Gurnah, "The Politics of Racism Awareness Training."

that view; as it registers only 22 publications that have cited Bidol's "Developing New Perspectives on Race," but 723 that have cited Katz's *White Awareness*.[10] Katz's work was also the basis of Racism Awareness Training's spread to the United Kingdom, where the UK government's Racism Awareness Programme Unit (RAPU) ran trainings in her style.[11]

What allowed *White Awareness* to stand out as a landmark publication in the field of Racism Awareness Training appears to have been its flexible structure. Unlike Terry's curricula, aimed exclusively at industry, or Bidol's, aimed exclusively at high-school students and teachers, Katz's program targeted a much broader audience:

> This program can be used and applied in many contexts and formats, depending upon the setting and the time limitations. The key to an effective program is to maintain flexibility and adaptability. A little imagination and knowledge of the group's needs is vital. The more the content of the program focuses on issues that reflect the participants' world, the more investment they will probably make, and the greater will be the degree of learning. Whether you are working with teachers, business people, counselors, administrators, students, church groups, or government officials, the program is easily adaptable. Some of the exercises presented in the handbook were geared to a university setting as only one example of the program's many applications. It has been adapted

---

10. Google, "Google Scholar 'Developing New Perspectives on Race.'"
    Google, "Google Scholar 'Whte Awareness.'"
11. Sivanandan, "RAT and the Degradation of Black Struggle," 153.

and used as part of Affirmative Action programs; in school systems with teachers, counselors, and administrators; in university settings with students, faculty, and dormitory staffs. ... The program has been used in various formats, ranging from three-hour introductory sessions to forty-five-hour semester-long university courses.[12]

The depth and sophistication of Katz's empirical analysis of her program's effectiveness also set her apart from Bidol and Terry. Her 1975 dissertation used data to demonstrate that her training program was effective in changing the attitudes and behaviors of attendees at least eight weeks after their session.[13] While the sample size was small (only 24 students), a follow-up study by Katz and her colleague Allen Ivey found that a full year after their re-education program "participants had become actively engaged in developing new curricula for schools, eliminating racism from their language, taking active roles in the governance of their organizations, examining criteria for hiring, facilitating workshops on racial awareness, and educating friends, families, and co-workers."[14]

Katz remains active to this day, working as an organizational development consultant in her role as Executive Vice President of the Kaleel Jameson Consulting Group, and sitting on the Dean's Council at her alma mater, the College of Education at the University of Massachusetts, Amherst.[15]

Katz served on the Board of Directors for another group that

---

12. Katz, *White Awareness*, 1978, 27-28.
13. Katz, "A Systematic Handbook of Exercises for the Re-Education of White People with Respect to Racist Attitudes and Behaviors," 40-67 and 296-327.
14. Katz and Ivey, "White Awareness," 489.
    Katz, *White Awareness*, 1978, 5.
15. Kaleel Jamison Consulting Group, Inc., "Judith H. Katz."

remains in operation, The Center for Study of White American Culture (CSWAC), an organization whose name is so reminiscent of a white supremacist organization that it has had to dedicate a whole page on their website to dispel that misconception.[16] Edler also served as an advisor and contributor to the organization.[17] CSWAC has specifically quoted Martin Luther King, Jr.'s "I Have A Dream" speech for the purpose of arguing against King and his claim that people should "not be judged by the color of their skin but by the content of their character."[18] CSWAC runs workshops on topics such as "Why Color Matters: From Colorblindness to Color Consciousness," "Raising Anti-Racist White Children," and "White Accountability and Organizing," all taught in the tradition of Terry, Bidol, Della-Dora, Edler, and Katz.[19]

CSWAC is hardly alone in teaching in the most radical incarnation of that tradition; Everyday Feminism is another organization still teaching it as well, running workshops for whites under names such as "Healing from Internalized Whiteness," teaching how to liberate oneself and others from the psychological and sociological impacts of living with "prejudice plus power."[20] Everyday Feminism advertises that their trainings have been used by government organizations including the Environmental Protection

---

16. Katz on board of directors from Center for the Study of White American Culture, Inc., "Center for the Study of White American Culture Membership Newsletter," 2.

"Misconceptions" page at Center for the Study of White American Culture, Inc., "Misconceptions about CSWAC."

17. Thanks to Edler from Hitchcock and Flint, "Decentering Whiteness," 2.

Blog contribution at Edler, "Transitions & White Anti-Racism."

18. Center for the Study of White American Culture, Inc., "Nate on Why Color Matters."

19. List of workshops: Center for the Study of White American Culture, Inc., "Workshops."

20. Everyday Feminism, "Healing from Internalized Whiteness 3-Day Training."

Everyday Feminism, "Healing from Internalized Whiteness," 7.

Agency, the City of Nashville, universities including the University of Colorado Boulder, Brown University, University of Pennsylvania, and Northwestern University, more mainstream progressive political organizations such as the Center on Budget and Policy Priorities, Act Blue, and Priorities USA, non-profits including OXFAM, and businesses including Wells Fargo.[21]

There are still many organizations, like CSWAC and Everyday Feminism, that conduct their trainings using explicitly radical language. However, the most successful organizations and individuals in this field today are those that have successfully taken the same fundamental concepts taught by Terry, Bidol, Della-Dora, Edler, and Katz and repackaged them to appear benign, agreeable, and academically credible.[22]

---

21. Everyday Feminism, "Beyond Diversity."
22. For just a few other examples of radical white on white anti-racist education, see the Coalition of Anti-Racist Whites and Whites for Racial Equity.

Robin DiAngelo and the Present Day

W hile others in the field of Critical Whiteness Studies have been influential in spreading white-on-white anti-racism—see Peggy McIntosh and Barbara Applebaum in particular—no one else has come close to having as seismic an impact as Robin DiAngelo.[1]

---

1. For more see McIntosh's highly cited paper "White Privilege: Unpacking the Invisible Knapsack" and Barbara Applebaum's 2010 book *Being White, Being Good: White Complicity, White Moral Responsibility, and Social Justice Pedagogy*. McIntosh was familiar with Katz, recommending people read her in Mcintosh, *On Privilege*, 211.

Applebaum's book is centered on explaining "the white complicity claim," meaning "that white people, through the practices of whiteness and by benefiting from white privilege, contribute to the maintenance of systemic racial injustice." Interestingly, Applebaum, as with Bidol and others before her, explicitly does that by redefining each key word necessary to make that claim analytically true from "complicity" all the way down. Applebaum explains: "I endeavor to elucidate what white complicity means when critical scholars of race and racism refer to it. A key task of this book is to demarcate some of the required moves that must be made in our conceptual landscape to make white complicity visible—in particular, shifts in our conceptualization of the subject, of language, and of moral responsibility." Applebaum, *Being White*, Chapter 1.

Robin DiAngelo received her PhD in Multicultural Education from the University of Washington in Seattle, focusing on "Whiteness Studies and Critical Discourse Analysis."[2] Her most famous book, *White Fragility: Why It's So Hard for White People to Talk About Racism*, spent a whopping 155 weeks on the New York Times Paperback Nonfiction Best Sellers list and 33 weeks on the overall Nonfiction Best Sellers list as of September 12, 2021, including multiple weeks in the number one spot.[3] It has been translated into eleven languages.[4] DiAngelo appeared on NBC News, MSNBC, CBS This Morning, CBS Primetime, NPR, PBS Newshour, CNN, and The Tonight Show with Jimmy Fallon, to name only a few, appearing on some programs multiple times. She and the book were profiled by many of the most notable newspapers in the country including The New York Times, USA Today, the Chicago Tribune, the Wall Street Journal, the Washington Post, Newsweek, the Atlantic, Vox, and more. The book even blew up in the sports world, being recommended by both ESPN and the NBA.[5] Having achieved anti-racist superstardom, DiAngelo became a highly sought-after public speaker; she requested (and was often given) tens of thousands of dollars in speaking fees for individual engagements.[6]

Another major entry of Racism Awareness Training's ideology into the 2020s was when in May of 2020, as the unrest in the aftermath of the killing of George Floyd was just starting, the Smithsonian's National Museum of African American History &

2. RobinDiAngelo.com, "About Me."
3. New York Times, "Paperback Nonfiction Books - Best Sellers."
    New York Times, "Combined Print & E-Book Nonfiction - Best Sellers."
4. RobinDiAngelo.com, "Publications."
5. Beacon Press, "Beacon Press: White Fragility."
6. Eberhart, "Anti-Racist Author DOUBLES Speaking Fees as America Goes Woke."

Culture published an infographic called the "Aspects and Assumptions of White Culture in the United States" intended to list supposedly white cultural traits, a few of which include "self-reliance," "objective, rational linear thinking," and "hard work is the key to success." The chart was based directly on Judith Katz's work.[7]

---

7.   National Museum of African American History & Culture, "Whiteness."

Alongside the chart on the museum's website read the following: "Data Source: 'Some Aspects and Assumptions of White Culture in the United States,' by Judith H. Katz, ©1990."

The chart was massively controversial, sparking outrage across conservative media, and eventually getting big enough to where even The Washington Post, Newsweek, and The Wall Street Journal covered it.[8] The National Museum of African American History & Culture eventually took down the graphic in response to the controversy. But the "whiteness" page where it formerly resided is still up; it features a 22-minute lecture by Robin DiAngelo and a substantial written discussion of her concept of "White Fragility."[9]

Beverly Daniel Tatum, an African American psychologist, educator, and former president of Spelman College, praised DiAngelo for her follow-up book to *White Fragility, Nice Racism: How Progressive White People Perpetuate Racial Harm*. On the book's front cover, Tatum admonishes potential buyers that "if you want to get beyond feeling defensive and increase your capacity for effective anti-racist action, do yourself a favor and read this book!" In her own bestselling book, *Why Are All the Black Kids Sitting Together in the Cafeteria?: And Other Conversations About Race*, Tatum notes how essential Katz's *White Awareness* handbook was

---

8. McGlone, "African American Museum Site Removes 'Whiteness' Chart after Criticism from Trump Jr. And Conservative Media."

Watts, "In Smithsonian Race Guidelines, Rational Thinking and Hard Work Are White Values."

Woodson, "The Resilience of the Black American."

9. National Museum of African American History & Culture, "Whiteness."

in helping her develop one of the first courses she taught on racism.[10] DiAngelo cited Tatum's book in her PhD dissertation.[11]

DiAngelo does not cite Katz, Terry, Della-Dora, Bidol, or Edler in any of her publicly available works.[12] However, DiAngelo's ideas are so strikingly similar to those developed by these theorists years earlier that her decision not to cite any of them could arguably be described as plagiarism. *White Fragility* is indistinguishable in its ideology and many of its arguments from Terry's *For Whites Only*. The entirety of DiAngelo's case in *White Fragility* rests on her rejection of the dictionary definition of "racism" in favor of a definition that is practically identical to Bidol's. In chapter one, DiAngelo writes that "if your definition of a racist is someone who

---

10. Tatum, *Why Are All the Black Kids Sitting Together in the Cafeteria?*, 73.

Tatum also cited NTL's Kurt Lewin on page 75.

Tatum herself serves as another major vector for Katz's transmission to the modern day. *Why Are All the Black Kids Sitting Together in the Cafeteria?* has appeared on book recommendation lists from the American Psychological Association, Forbes, USA Today, NPR, the New York Post, and the National Association of Independent Schools (NAIS). Tatum's work on "White Identity Development" has also been used by the NAIS and the major national non-profit education consultancy Pollyanna, Inc.

American Psychological Association usage from American Psychological Association, "Books about Race and Ethnicity."

Forbes usage from Wuench, "First, Listen. Then, Learn: Anti-Racism Resources for White People."

USA Today usage from Reed and Yasharoff, "Looking for Books about Racism? Experts Suggest These Must-Read Titles for Adults and Kids."

NPR usage from Rosario, "This List of Books, Films and Podcasts about Racism Is a Start, Not a Panacea."

New York Post usage from Cost, "7 Books about Racism Every Adult Should Read Right Now."

NAIS usage from Lai to attendees of Facilitating Courageous Conversations Visually seminar, "NAIS PoCC Seminar | Part 2 Recording + Other Things."

Pollyanna usage from Seibert to eSeminar Participants, "NYSAIS: RACE TALK IS DIVIDING US! And Other Myths about Race and Racial Literacy Curriculum in K-12 Schools."

11. DiAngelo, "Whiteness in Racial Dialogue: A Discourse Analysis," 264.

12. RobinDiAngelo.com, "Publications."

holds conscious dislike of people because of race, then I agree that it is offensive for me to suggest that you are racist when I don't know you. I also agree that if this is your definition of racism, and you are against racism, then you are not racist. Now breathe. I am not using this definition of racism."[13] Instead she taught, as did those before her, that "to understand racism, we need to first distinguish it from mere prejudice and discrimination. ... When a racial group's collective prejudice is backed by the power of legal authority and institutional control, it is transformed into racism ... When I say that only whites can be racist, I mean that in the United States, only whites have the collective social and institutional power and privilege over people of color."[14] Moreover, DiAngelo's title concept of "white fragility" is itself a restatement of Edler's "distancing behaviors," a "kafkatrap" in which any attempt to deny that one has white fragility or that one is distancing is in itself an example of one participating in white fragility or distancing.[15]

DiAngelo's suggestions on how *White Fragility* should be used in an educational setting are also reminiscent of her predecessors. In the "Reading Guide" for *White Fragility*, DiAngelo on the very first page identifies "distancing" as a common pattern to be avoided; some of the examples she gives of distancing patterns are identical to Edler's. She also advised running a discussion group with "facilitators" merely serving "as guides rather than as teachers," and helping people reach certain predetermined conclusions within the group discussion–the same group dynamics techniques used by

---

13. DiAngelo, *White Fragility*, Chapter 1.

14. DiAngelo, *White Fragility*, Chapter 2.
    Interestingly, DiAngelo cites this view to no one at all, speaking purely from her own alleged authority.

15. For more on white fragility as a kafkatrap see Burke, "The Intellectual Fraud of Robin DiAngelo's 'White Fragility.'"

NTL in their trainings and proposed by Katz in *White Awareness*.[16] Many of the guide's group discussion exercises were identical to those in Bidol and Katz's curricula, including asking participants to discuss "the difference between racial prejudice, racial discrimination, and racism," and, as with Katz's curriculum, with the correct answer predetermined.[17]

The Reading Guide claimed that "this book and its arguments build on antiracism scholarship and activism that people of color have written for generations," a statement somewhere between misleading and false given how directly it hewed to material created for white people by white people.[18] But the claim is informative of how DiAngelo gained her success and representative of her techniques.

For all the controversy that DiAngelo achieved on her own, imagine how soundly her ideas might have been rejected had people known the full story of where they came from.

---

16. DiAngelo and Sensoy, *Reading Guide for White Fragility*, 1-3.

   Katz, *White Awareness*, 1978, 25.

   DiAngelo refers to these groups as white "affinity groups,", affinity groups having become popular in businesses and educational institutions as social and working groups based on member identity. To what extent all affinity groups share their methods and origin in NTL techniques remains an open question worthy of investigation.

17. DiAngelo and Sensoy, *Reading Guide for White Fragility*, 6.

18. DiAngelo and Sensoy, *Reading Guide for White Fragility*, 4.

Conclusion

The "Power + Prejudice" redefinition has seriously threatened the liberal idea of treating everyone as individuals rather than as members of identity groups. However, by understanding its history, we can debunk a number of claims made by modern proponents of the redefinition:

> 1. **The "Power + Prejudice" redefinition is not the product of credible academic study; it and other redefinitions were contrived by far-left activists to forward their revolutionary worldview.**

Today, the redefinition is often given academic credibility it does not deserve. In multiple instances, including one from Britain's "newspaper of record" The Telegraph, Bidol has been misremembered as a "social scientist."[1] Calling her a social scientist

---

1. Bidol as social scientist from Wilkinson, "What Is It About the Left Which

is misleading at best as it implies that a level of scientific rigor went into creating the redefinition. At the time, Bidol was a high school educator, not a social scientist. Similarly, Delmo Della-Dora's doctorate was in education.[2] Judith Katz, who was the most prominent spreader of the definition in the 1970s, earned an EdD from the University of Massachusetts.

In 1973, Terry earned a PhD, but in divinity. His dissertation, the basis of much of what was written here, was a history of the Detroit Industrial Mission. Carmichael's highest degree was a bachelor's degree, and while being the most remembered subject of this book, he is not remembered as an academic, although his co-author Charles V. Hamilton became a professor of political science two years after the publication of *Black Power*.[3]

Regardless, today it is extraordinarily rare to hear any of these names tied to the "Power + Prejudice" redefinition; instead, the redefinition is erroneously assumed to be academic in nature and is frequently taught as such in academia. The already-fallacious appeal to authority—claiming that the redefinition is correct because it was created by "experts"—falls apart entirely upon looking at the many incorrect and fringe beliefs those "experts" held. Even actual academics who use the "Power + Prejudice" definition of racism in their work are unlikely to be familiar with its origins. Bidol's curriculum is available in only seven libraries worldwide, and fewer still have the original 1970 edition.[4]

Thus, those teaching the redefinition today and its associated

---

Makes Anti-Semitism so Common?" See also Dunst, "Progressives Have a New Definition of Racism"; and Estrada-Salazar, "No, Racism Is Not Prejudice plus Power."

Telegraph as "newspaper of record" from Martin and Hansen, "Newspapers of Record in a Digital Age."

2. Obituary Department, "Delmo Della-Dora."
3. Carmichael and Hamilton, *Black Power*, From the Authors.
4. Worldcat, "Developing New Perspectives on Race."

views within Racism Awareness Training are simply parroting successful activism. There's nothing necessarily wrong with being an activist, so long as one is forthcoming about their activism. Employees don't expect to be hearing from activists when their companies bring in corporate anti-racism trainers; they expect to be hearing from unbiased experts. Similarly with students in school. Treating activists as if they are experts who have the singular perspective that can possibly be considered correct is fraudulent and unfortunately now widespread.

2. The activist's worldview often rejects the actual opinions of black people, yet it falsely claims to represent the interests of the entire black community.

When Joseph Hudson put together the New Detroit Committee, he gave disproportionate representation to militant activists, despite polls that demonstrated these views were widely unpopular with black people. When Delmo Della-Dora put together MOREL's programs, he justified ignoring the majority black viewpoint on the grounds that "only a minority of Negroes perceive 'the black experience' in our society through black eyes."[5]

Since then, the practice of disregarding black public opinion when convenient has only gotten worse. Nikole Hannah-Jones, founder of the New York Times's 1619 Project, has argued that "there is a difference between being racially black and politically black," in essence claiming that black people aren't really black unless they share her brand of politics.[6] This position is grounded in radical academic theories that argue an "authentic black voice" must

---

5. Della-Dora, *Planning New Development Efforts Recommended Procedures,* 11
6. Richardson, "Architect of NYT's 1619 Project Draws Distinction."

agree with these theories, thus erasing the majority of black Americans who are not political radicals.[7] It is allegedly impossible to authentically have a difference of opinion as these unfalsifiable theories argue that disagreement is simply "false consciousness."[8] This position broke into Racism Awareness Training through the work of James Edler.

Black people are not a monolith, nor are members of any race. All racial groups are made up of individuals. To say that every individual in a racial group must hold the same perspective is itself racist. Although horrible and racist when one black person tells another black person how they must act and think in order to be authentically black, it intuitively seems even worse when a white person makes the same claim. Racism Awareness Training in the tradition of Della-Dora does exactly that.

The only way to be an "anti-racist racist" in this philosophy is to follow its fringe radical viewpoint in full. Otherwise, one is simply a "racist racist." But there are real disagreements in the black community. In the wake of the murder of George Floyd, as nationwide protests, media coverage, and riots called to "defund the police," 50 percent of black Americans still believed "we need more cops on the street," and 50 percent believed the opposite.[9] Is it at all reasonable, given this information, to say that anyone who doesn't support Black Lives Matter's activism to "defund the police" and to "abolish police and prisons" is negligent in the fight to end racism and thus a racist?[10]

There are legitimate differences of opinion on how we can most effectively fight racism. The far-left position, as outlined in this book, is fringe in the black community; but so are conservative positions. A

---

7. New Discourses, "Authentic."
8. New Discourses, "False Consciousness."
9. Klein, *How Can I Be a Good Ally in the Fight for Social Justice?*
10. Woodson, "Why Conservatives Have a Problem with Black Lives Matter."

position being fringe or mainstream has little connection to whether it is right or wrong. But so long as black people hold a diversity of viewpoints—as they do—it is both counter-productive and false to condemn as racists would-be white allies in the fight for racial justice if they don't adopt an entire radical worldview.

3. **Establishment actors often separate radical ideas from their radical roots, providing them with a falsely mainstream appearance.**

When the United States Commission on Civil Rights published *Racism In America and How to Combat It*, it provided the appearance of mainstream legitimacy to the ideas of Stokely Carmichael. How? It didn't tell readers the true source of the ideas it contained and what those ideas were designed to do. We know from the commissioners' concluding statements that at least one of them felt the need to clarify "I am opposed to black racism, white racism, and racism in any form wherever it is found."[11] Would he have still supported the publication had he known that the originator of these ideas admitted that "in the end, we cannot and shall not offer any guarantees that Black Power, if achieved, would be non-racist. ... If black racism is what the larger society fears, we cannot help them"?[12] Similarly, would the New Detroit Speakers' Bureau have succeeded in reaching at least 188,000 people without the veneer of credibility granted to it as an organization founded by the governor, mayor, and business leaders?

This same mechanism continues today, and not just as it relates to fighting racism. Often good ideas can come from radical people. Someone being "extreme" is not, in itself, a sufficient reason to

---

11. U.S. Commission on Civil Rights, *Racism in America and How to Combat It*, 42
12. Carmichael and Hamilton, *Black Power*, 45

discard their arguments. But the agenda for introducing those ideas doesn't disappear just because it isn't mentioned. Downs didn't mention that one of the implications of the ideas he laundered was that it could actually end up causing *more* racism rather than ending racism of all types once and for all, as is the end goal of "colorblind" anti-racists. The Detroit Industrial Mission didn't mention to companies that their end goal was socialism and revolution, but that agenda still remains even if it's not mentioned. Those continuing the Racism Awareness Trainings that DIM started may or may not know about that agenda, but nonetheless it remains true that the views they spread are calibrated to lead there.

Look at Carmichael's definition of "institutional racism." Because he defines it in a way that deems any unequal outcomes along racial lines to be examples of racism, it is self-contained in the definition that the defeat of institutional racism will result in the rise of equalitarian communism. But do most of the people today talking about institutional racism know that? Have they thought it all way through? Certainly not—although there is a powerful minority of activists who do understand its full implications.[13] Nonetheless, the masses provide political pressure to move in that direction, unaware that they are doing so.

All the redefinitions of racism mentioned in this writing create exactly this phenomenon, each with different nuances. The redefinitions bake so much into the concept of "racism" that adopting that definition necessarily means adopting a much larger political framework. All of us except the true racists want to fight racism. Deceiving people into adopting an entire set of radical politics in the name of fighting "racism" is a cynical and manipulative maneuver. Unfortunately, it's also very effective.

---

13. See Black Lives Matter's calls to end capitalism here: Woodson, "Why Conservatives Have a Problem with Black Lives Matter."

4. **Understand the impact of letting the extremists in.**

Good intentions lead good people to try to stop bad things; they're not always smart about how they try.

In New Detroit, efforts to hear from all points of view and end rioting led leadership to welcome in militant extremists. Was it worth it? In the decades that have followed, have the actions described from New Detroit led to more racial harmony or less? Shortly following the death of George Floyd, Senator Mitt Romney (R-UT) repeated the errors of his father, marching with Black Lives Matter protestors and tweeting "Black Lives Matter."[14] To be clear, black lives do matter, and police brutality is a serious issue. Senator Romney had plainly good intentions. But without addressing the extreme views of the official Black Lives Matter organization and its chapters (which were founded by trained Marxists, supported Fidel Castro, and explicitly want to abolish capitalism, the nuclear family, police, and prisons) Romney provided them an avenue to grow their legitimacy and influence.[15] Governor George Romney had similarly good intentions when he established New Detroit, but it ultimately turned into a platform for people like Bidol to spread a divisive philosophy that has harmed our fight for racial harmony.

Of course, the extremists don't see their views as futile, but they do understand the importance of leveraging mainstream support to forward them. The Detroit Industrial Mission's "inside/outside" strategy is an example. DIM had an uphill battle in gaining access to industry. When it started, it didn't have a brand of legitimate expertise; the natural reaction to it was skepticism and fear it would organize labor against the company. Regardless of one's view on the

---

14. Romney, "Black Lives Matter."
15. Woodson, "Why Conservatives Have a Problem with Black Lives Matter."

virtues of unionization, why should any company willingly let in people they perceive as harmful to their business? But over time, it achieved increasing access to industry. It didn't push any radical views at all until the riots changed everything. Quickly companies had a new awareness of the need to fight racism, and DIM had services to offer. DIM's staff were able to successfully position themselves as experts and spread their ideology. But unbeknownst to the companies as a whole, DIM had no intention of simply educating them for minor change. DIM wanted radical change. It used its trainings to prepare corporate insiders to aid a potentially violent revolution outside. What DIM would push late in its existence would be much worse than what industry feared DIM would push in its early years.

Today, the effects of letting extremists influence corporations are mixed. On the one hand, dozens of companies donated to the official Black Lives Matter Global Network organization, but on the other hand, few are becoming socialist co-ops. Efforts to placate social justice activists have mostly been minor PR efforts, although even that dangerously emboldens their societal influence. But specific types of corporations and other organizations have been more heavily impacted. Universities now have entire departments dedicated to teaching these ideas, and they are actively influencing the rest of the academy. Some journalistic publications have been entirely conquered; for example, *Teen Vogue*, which started as a fashion magazine, has, in more recent years, explicitly promoted Karl Marx and communism.[16]

Once extremists have access, they attempt to get what they want. Why wouldn't they? Unless your organization fully agrees with those ideas, keep them out, or you will regret it, exactly as the United States Military did.

---

16. Corcione, "Everything You Should Know About Karl Marx."

5. **Don't miss the Motte & Bailey; "anti-racism" is a loaded term. Don't let extremists misrepresent themselves.**

Sometimes it can be hard to keep the extremists out, as they often have a vested interest in portraying themselves as less radical than they truly are. As seen in MOREL's public relations efforts after being called out for the details of Hurwitz & Snook's program, the defense of radical ideas is often couched in the language of uncontroversial ideas. All good people care about fighting racism, and in that sense, most Americans are "anti-racist." If we hear that there is an effort to fight racism, our instinct is to support it. What are we to do when those flying the flag of "anti-racism" are actually racists who support treating people differently based on the color of their skin? What do we do when the "racism" that they oppose is actually an unusual and strategically invented definition that doesn't mean what most of their audience takes it to mean?

The new "anti-racists'" victory in the language game is a major coup. Is there any question whether they could have spread their philosophy so successfully had they named it "neo-segregationism?" Of course not. A common mistake of those who oppose these self-described "anti-racists" is to declare that they oppose "anti-racism." To the minority of well-informed people, this makes perfect sense, but what about those who aren't as familiar with the radical ideology behind the new "anti-racists?" If they see people opposing "anti-racism" writ large, their reasonable presumption will be that those people are racists. They'll come to believe racism is a bigger problem in society than it actually is, given they are coming across racists in their lives where they had previously never noticed them, and be pushed further into the arms of the "anti-racists."

So how do we win against these radicals? Our first step must be to regain control of the language. We are the true anti-racists. They are anti-integrationists (at best) and neo-segregationists (at worst). We gain nothing by giving up the term anti-racist, which is the accurate description of what we are and an inaccurate description of what they are. We have the moral high ground; we have the actual, proven solutions to racial discrimination and prejudice. There's no reason we shouldn't look like it too.

Many who spread the "Power + Prejudice" redefinition today argue that we must pay *more* attention to race—instead of less, as Martin Luther King, Jr. famously dreamed—because racial inequities still exist and to ignore race (being "colorblind") prevents us from noticing and fighting them.[17] They concede that a day might eventually come when equality is achieved, but that until then, colorblind anti-racism will only further instill racism.[18] But this begs the question: when will we finally achieve equality of outcome? Ibram X. Kendi, New York Times bestselling author and "anti-racist" academic who has successfully courted multi-million-dollar donations, argues that we need a constitutional amendment enshrining that "racial inequity is evidence of racist policy" and founding an unaccountable, omnipotent "Department of Anti-Racism" to enforce that principle.[19] In Kendi's view, any amount of unequal outcomes between races is enough to prevent judging people by their character instead of their color.

Never mind that *any* two groups you measure will have different outcomes. Among white Americans of different heritages, on average, Australian Americans have a higher income than Russian Americans, who have a higher income than French Americans.[20] Does that mean Australian Americans are using institutional racism

---

17. Tochluk, "Why Pay Attention to Race."
18. See this example, which had its comments section shut down due to criticism: Williams, "Colorblind Ideology Is a Form of Racism."
19. White, "Jack Dorsey Donates $10 Million to a Group."
20. Klein, *Oppression Can't Be Measured by Outcome.*

against French Americans to cause that inequality? Should we encourage Australian vs. French identity politics to correct this imbalance? Would we ever succeed in creating that balance? Or would any effort to equalize these groups in all metrics inevitably fail, and further divide America in the process?

Such pure equalitarianism is not achievable, and where it was tried, it led to political authoritarianism, mass poverty, and, in the worst cases, millions of deaths. Stokely Carmichael believed it was possible and desirable; and whether they realize it or not, those who are forwarding his ideas today are also forwarding his radical equalitarian philosophy. It cannot ever succeed, but as history has shown us, its zealous adherents can do a lot of damage in their attempts to make it work.

The only thing standing in the way of racial harmony is bad ideas, and "Power + Prejudice" is a devastatingly bad idea. If tomorrow everyone stopped treating people differently based on the color of their skin, King's dream would be achieved. You can be a part of trendy activism, or you can be a part of a true solution.

I refuse to determine what is right by taking a Gallup poll of the trends of the time. I imagine that there were leaders in Germany who sincerely opposed what Hitler was doing to the Jews. But they took their poll and discovered that antiSemitism was the prevailing trend. In order to "be in step with the times," in order to "keep in touch," they yielded to one of the most ignominious evils that history has ever known.

Ultimately a genuine leader is not a searcher for consensus but a molder of consensus. I said on one occasion, "If every Negro in the United States turns to violence, I will choose to be that one lone voice preaching that this is the wrong way." Maybe this sounded like arrogance. But it was not intended that way. It was simply my way of saying that I would rather be a man of conviction than a man of conformity. Occasionally in life one develops a conviction so precious and meaningful that he will stand on it till the end.[21]

— Martin Luther King Jr.

---

21. King, *Where Do We Go from Here?*, 65–66

Acknowledgments

I want to acknowledge the assistance of Jared Cummings, Patrick Esch, Caleb Sutherlin, Harry Kazenoff, Jonathan Harsh, Jonathan Gonzalez, and Chris O'Neil in researching this, the Capital Research Center and Scott Walter for providing me with the freedom and flexibility to dedicate so much time to this story, Jon Rodeback, Colin Wright, Grayson Slover, and Dana Stangel-Plowe for editing, Professor Daniel B. Klein for his feedback and suggestions, and most of all my friend and colleague Dr. Steven J. Allen, who taught me how to perform all the research necessary and without whom this book could not exist.

Works Cited

Agee, Phil Jr. "The National Student Association Scandal." Campus Watch, Fall 1991. http://www.namebase.net:82/campus/nsa2.html.

Ahmad, A. Muhammad. "League of Revolutionary Black Workers: A Historical Study." History Is a Weapon. https://www.historyisaweapon.com/defcon1/rbwstudy.html.

American Psychiatric Association. *Diagnostic and Statistical Manual of Mental Disorders: DSM-5*. Arlington, VA: 2013.

American Psychological Association. "Books about Race and Ethnicity." Apa.org. March 2018. https://www.apa.org/res/parent-resources/books.

American University. "Patricia Bidol-Padva Bio." American University. https://www.american.edu/spa/faculty/bidolpad.cfm

Anthony, Andrew. "Black Power's Coolest Radicals (but Also a Gang of Ruthless Killers)." *Guardian*, October 18, 2015. https://www.theguardian.com/film/2015/oct/18/black-powers-coolest-radicals-black-panthers-vanguard-of-the-revolution-stanley-nelson-interview.

Applebaum, Barbara. *Being White, Being Good: White Complicity, White Moral Responsibility, and Social Justice Pedagogy*. Lanham, MD: Lexington Books, 2010.

Applegate, Beth. "Member Mondays: Beth Applegate." Monroe County National Organization for Women, July 3, 2017. https://www.monroecountynow.org/blog/2017/6/26/member-mondays-rachel-guglielmo-6rwhs

AR Staff. "Sam Francis in His Own Words." American Renaissance, December 28, 2019. https://www.amren.com/news/2011/02/sam_francis_in/.

Army Infantry School. *Race Relations Orientation Packet for Leaders*. Fort Benning, GA: Department of the Army, 1973.

Batista, Ed (@edbatista). "If you're interested in T-groups, humanistic psychology, the craziness of the late '60s, and/or Cold War paranoia, read on." Twitter, February 22, 2020, 10:41 a.m. https://twitter.com/edbatista/status/1231242555997577218.

BBC News "'Mass Graves' Found in Guinea." BBC, October 22, 2002. http://news.bbc.co.uk/2/hi/africa/2349639.stm.

Beacon Press. "Beacon Press: White Fragility." http://www.beacon.org/White-Fragility-P1631.aspx.

Bernstein, David. "Sorry, but the Irish Were Always 'White' (and so Were Italians,

Jews and so On)." Washington Post, March 22, 2017. https://www.washingtonpost.com/news/volokh-conspiracy/wp/2017/03/22/sorry-but-the-irish-were-always-white-and-so-were-the-italians-jews-and-so-on/.

Bidol, Pat A. *Developing New Perspectives on Race: An Innovative Multi-Media Social Studies Curriculum in Race Relations for the Secondary Level*. Revised Edition. Detroit, Michigan: New Perspectives on Race, 1972.

Bidol, Patricia A. *Developing New Perspectives on Race: An Innovative Multi-Media Social Studies Curriculum in Race Relations for the Secondary Level*. Detroit, Michigan: New Detroit Inc., 1970.

Bidol, Patricia A. LinkedIn, 2020. https://www.linkedin.com/in/pat-bidol-padva-ph-d-94b173a/.

Bidol, Patricia A. "Mini-Lecture on Differences Between Prejudice and Racism." People Acting Together for Change (PACT), Detroit, MI.

Bidol, Patricia Ann Fitzsimmons. "The Effects of Racism Awareness Training on the Staff of an Educational Association." 1972.

Biography.com Editors. "Angela Davis Biography." Biography.com, October 18, 2020. https://www.biography.com/activist/angela-davis.

Bloom, Joshua, and Waldo E. Martin Jr. *Black Against Empire: The History and Politics of the Black Panther Party*. Oakland, CA: University of California Press, 2016.

Boudry, Maarten, and John Braeckman. "Immunizing Strategies and Epistemic Defense Mechanisms." *Philosophia* 39, no. 1 (2010): 145–161. https://doi.org/10.1007/s11406-010-9254-9.

Bradford, Leland P. *National Training Laboratories: Its History 1947–1970*. National Institute for Applied Behavioral Science, 1974.

Bryant, Bunyan, Janet C. Huber, and Debra K. Stowe. *Resources for School Change: III. A Manual on Issues and Strategies in Resource Utilization*. US Department of Health, Education and Welfare, 1972. https://files.eric.ed.gov/fulltext/ED069046.pdf.

Burgin, Sarah Nicole. "'The Most Progressive and Forward Looking Race Relations Experiment in Existence': Race 'Militancy', Whiteness, and DRRI in the Early 1970s." *Journal of American Studies* 49, no. 3 (2014). https://doi.org/10.1017/s0021875814001856.

Burgin, Sarah Nicole. "The Workshop as the Work: White Anti-Racism Organizing in 1960s, 70s, and 80s Social Movements." Ph.D. dissertation, University of Leeds, 2013.

Burgin, Say. "Locating Douglass Fitch: The Roots of Colour and Activist Traditions of United States Critical Whiteness Studies." University of Leeds, 2013.

Burke, David. "The Intellectual Fraud of Robin DiAngelo's 'White Fragility.'"

Medium, June 24, 2020. https://medium.com/@thelogicalliberal/the-intellectual-fraud-of-robin-diangelos-white-fragility-e98197d16eb1.

Callahan, John. "A History of the Esalen Institute." Steven K. Harper, 2012.

Camp, Frank. "Democratic Strategist Claims Sarah Jeong Tweets Aren't Racist Because Racism Is 'Prejudice Plus Power.'" Daily Wire, August 4, 2018. https://www.dailywire.com/news/democratic-strategist-claims-sarah-jeong-tweets-frank-camp.

Carmichael, Stokely, and Charles V. Hamilton. *Black Power*. Penguin Books, 1969.

Center for Resources on Institutional Oppression. Letter to Joint Strategy and Action Committee. "A Proposal from the Center for Resources on Institutional Oppression," February 23, 1973.

Center for the Study of White American Culture, Inc. "Center for the Study of White American Culture Membership Newsletter," 2000. https://www.euroamerican.org/Library/MemberNews/News2000_2_spring.pdf.

Center for the Study of White American Culture, Inc. "Misconceptions about CSWAC." Accessed January 3, 2022. https://cswac.org/about/misconceptions-about-cswac/.

Center for the Study of White American Culture, Inc. "Nate on Why Color Matters." YouTube.com, December 13, 2018. https://youtu.be/13JmGW4B1Sk.

Center for the Study of White American Culture, Inc. "Workshops." Accessed January 3, 2022. https://cswac.org/upcoming-workshops/.

Chen, Hans H. "LBJ Targeted Black Power Radicals: Files Show FBI Secretly Checked Stokely Carmichael's Draft Status." African-American Involvement in the Vietnam War, May 15, 2000. http://aavw.org/protest/carmichael_carmichael_abstract23.html.

City of Detroit Historic Designation Advisory Board. "Madison Office Building." HistoricDetroit.org. https://historicdetroit.org/buildings/madison-office-building.

Coghlan, David, and Claus Jacobs, "Kurt Lewin on Reeducation." NTL Institute, 2005.

Colding, Chuck. "Memo To: Lawrence P. Doss & Walter Douglass." Detroit, MI: Walter P. Reuther Library, New Detroit, Inc. Records UR000660, Box 172, Folder 24, September 4, 1973.

Coleman, James S. *Equality of Educational Opportunity*. National Center for Educational Statistics. 1966.

Columbia University Faculty. "Kimberlé Crenshaw on Intersectionality, More than Two Decades Later." Columbia Law School, June 8, 2017. https://www.law.columbia.edu/news/archive/kimberle-crenshaw-intersectionality-more-two-decades-later.

Congress, Senate, Committee on the Judiciary, *Testimony of Stokely Carmichael,*

United States Senate, 91st Congress, 2nd Session, March 25, 1970. History Matters, George Mason University. http://historymatters.gmu.edu/d/6461/.

Connell, William J., and Fred Gardaphé. *Anti-Italianism: Essays on a Prejudice.* New York: Palgrave Macmillan, 2010.

Conroy, Meredith, and Perry Bacon Jr. "There's a Huge Gap in How Republicans and Democrats See Discrimination." FiveThirtyEight, June 17, 2020. https://fivethirtyeight.com/features/theres-still-a-huge-partisan-gap-in-how-americans-see-discrimination/.

Cooperative Project for Educational Development. *Concepts for Social Change.* National Training Laboratories, 1967.

Corcione, Adryan. "Everything You Should Know About Karl Marx." Teen Vogue, May 10, 2018. https://www.teenvogue.com/story/who-is-karl-marx.

Cost, Ben. "7 Books about Racism Every Adult Should Read Right Now." *New York Post,* June 3, 2020. https://nypost.com/2020/06/03/7-books-about-racism-every-adult-should-read-right-now/.

Crosby, Robert P. "T-Group as Cutting Edge: Today? Really?" Crosby and Associates, 2013. https://www.pnodn.org/Resources/Documents/Speaker%20Resources/T%20as%20Cutting%20Edge%20-%20Final%20Our%20version.pdf

Daniels, Victor. "Kurt Lewin Notes." Sonoma State University, December 3, 2003. http://web.sonoma.edu/users/d/daniels/lewinnotes.html.

Defense Equal Opportunity Management Institute. "About DEOMI." DEOMI.org. https://www.deomi.org/about/history.cfm.

Defense Equal Opportunity Management Institute. *Defense Equal Opp Mgt FOIA.* Washington, DC: Judicial Watch, 2020. https://www.judicialwatch.org/wp-content/uploads/2020/07/Defense-Equal-Opp-Mgt-budget-1.pdf.

Della-Dora, Delmo. "Racism and Prejudice: How Did We Get This Way?" 1968.

Della-Dora, Delmo. "The Culturally Disadvantaged: Further Observations." *Exceptional Children* 29, no. 5 (January 1963). https://doi.org/10.1177/001440296302900506.

Della-Dora, Delmo. *Planning New Development Efforts Recommended Procedures.* Detroit, MI: Michigan-Ohio Regional Educational Laboratory, 1969.

Della-Dora, Delmo. *Racism and Education: A Review of Segregation, Discrimination, and Other Aspects of Racism in Education.* U.S. Department of Health, Education, and Welfare, Office of Education, and Michigan-Ohio Regional Education Lab. Detroit: May 1969.

Department of Defense. "No. 1322.11 Department of Defense Education in Race Relations for Armed Forces Personnel," June 24, 1971.

Department of the Army. "No. 600-42 Race Relations Education for the Army," February 1, 1974.

DiAngelo, Robin. "Deconstructing White Privilege with Robin DiAngelo." YouTube. General Commission on Religion and Race of the UMC, March 20, 2018. https://youtu.be/h7mzj0cVL0Q.

DiAngelo, Robin J. *White Fragility: Why It's So Hard for White People To Talk About Racism*. Boston, MA: Beacon Press, 2018.

DiAngelo, Robin J. "Whiteness in Racial Dialogue: A Discourse Analysis." 2004. https://www.nas.org/storage/app/media/New%20Documents/DiAngelo%20Dissertation%20-%202004.pdf.

DiAngelo, Robin, and Özlem Sensoy. *Reading Guide for White Fragility*. Boston, MA: Beacon Press. https://www.beacon.org/assets/pdfs/whitefragilityreadingguide.pdf.

Digital Gateway. "SNCC Staff Meeting at Peg Leg Bates Club." SNCC Digital Gateway. https://snccdigital.org/events/sncc-staff-meeting-peg-leg-bates-club/.

Digital Gateway. "Stokely Carmichael Elected as SNCC's Chair." SNCC Digital Gateway. https://snccdigital.org/events/stokely-carmichael-elected-snccs-chair/.

Dobbin, Frank, and Alexandra Kalev. "Why Doesn't Diversity Training Work? The Challenge for Academia." *Anthropology Now* 10, no. 2 (September 2018). https://scholar.harvard.edu/files/dobbin/files/an2018.pdf.

Doss, Lawrence P. "Recommendations to the Board of Trustees." New Detroit Inc. Project Advisory Committee, May 27, 1971.

Downs, Anthony. *An Economic Theory of Democracy*. New York: Harper and Roe, 1957.

Dunst, Charles. "Progressives Have a New Definition of Racism: 'Prejudice plus Power.'" New York Jewish Week, August 13, 2018. https://jewishweek.timesofisrael.com/progressives-have-a-new-definition-of-racism-prejudice-plus-power/.

Eberhart, Christopher. "Anti-Racist Author DOUBLES Speaking Fees as America Goes Woke: 'White Fragility' Writer Robin DiAngelo Charges an Average of $14,000 per Speech and Makes '$728K a Year.'" *Daily Mail*, July 2, 2021. https://www.dailymail.co.uk/news/article-9749517/An-anti-racist-author-Robin-DiAngelo-makes-728K-year-speaking-engagements.html.

Edler, James Merryweather. "White on White: An Anti-Racism Manual for White Educators in the Process of Becoming." EdD Diss., University of Massachusetts, January, 1974.

Edler, Jim. "Transitions & White Anti-Racism: Thoughts from a White Guy." Center for the Study of White American Culture, Inc., June 15, 2012. https://cswac.org/transitions-white-anti-racism-thoughts-from-a-white-guy/.

Edwards, Clifford H. "Sensitivity Training and Education: A Critique." Association for Supervision and Curriculum Development, 1970.

Edwards, Clifford H. *Educational Change: From Traditional Education to Learning Communities.* Lanham, MD: Rowman and Littlefield, January 16, 2011.

Encyclopædia Britannica. "Kurt Lewin." https://www.britannica.com/biography/Kurt-Lewin.

Encyclopædia Britannica. "Roy Wilkins." https://www.britannica.com/biography/Roy-Wilkins.

Encyclopædia Britannica. "Whitney M. Young, Jr." https://www.britannica.com/biography/Whitney-M-Young-Jr.

Encyclopædia Britannica. "Marcus Garvey: Jamaican Black Nationalist Leader."

Encyclopedia of Marxism. https://www.marxists.org/glossary/index.htm.

Estrada-Salazar, Christopher. "No, Racism Is Not Prejudice plus Power." *Student Life* (Claremont Colleges), March 14, 2019. https://tsl.news/opinion-no-racism-is-not-prejudice-plus-power/.

Everyday Feminism. "Beyond Diversity: How to Build a Truly Anti-Racist Organization." Everyday Feminism, May 25, 2018. https://everydayfeminism.com/build-anti-racist-organization/.

Everyday Feminism. "Healing from Internalized Whiteness." Flip chart at in-person training, January 16, 2019.

Everyday Feminism. "Healing from Internalized Whiteness 3-Day Training," October 7, 2018. https://everydayfeminism.com/healing-from-internalized-whiteness/.

Feuerherd, Peter. "When Christian Evangelicals Loved Socialism." JSTOR Daily, January 31, 2019. https://daily.jstor.org/when-christian-evangelicals-loved-socialism/.

Fine, Sidney. "Rioters and Judges: The Response of the Criminal Justice System to the Detroit Riot of 1967." *Wayne Law Review,* 1986–1987.

Fine, Sidney. *Violence in the Model City: The Cavanagh Administration, Race Relations, and the Detroit Riot of 1967.* Michigan State University Press, 2012.

Fitch, Douglas E. "Life & Work / Doing My Thing." *Detroit Industrial Mission* 11, no. 2 (February 1969).

Frankovic, Kathy. "Optimism Grows Among Black Americans That Protests Will Improve How Police Treat Them." YouGov, June 19, 2020. https://today.yougov.com/topics/politics/articles-reports/2020/06/19/optimism-grows-among-black-americans-over-protests.

Garrow, David J. "The Tragedy of Stokely Carmichael." *Reviews in American History* 43, no. 3 (September 2015). https://doi.org/10.1353/rah.2015.0075.

Georgakas, Dan, and Marvin Surkin. *Detroit: I Do Mind Dying: A Study in Urban Revolution*. Haymarket Books, 2012.

Gerard, Nathan. "'Marx Was Right': Lessons From Lewin." Society for Industrial and Organizational Psychology, April 1, 2017. https://www.siop.org/Research-Publications/Items-of-Interest/ArtMID/19366/ArticleID/1552/Marx-Was-Right-Lessons-From-Lewin.

Geschwender, James A. *Class, Race, and Worker Insurgency: The League of Revolutionary Black Workers*. Cambridge University Press, 1977.

Goldenberg, Ashley Rae. "Defense Department: The Bible, Constitution and Declaration of Independence All Perpetuate Sexism." Daily Caller, April 13, 2015. https://dailycaller.com/2015/04/13/defense-department-the-bible-constitution-and-declaration-of-independence-all-perpetuate-sexism/.

Google. "Google Books Ngram Viewer, 'racism, racialism.'" Google Books. https://books.google.com/ngrams/graph?content=racism,+racialism&year_start=1905&year_end=1975&corpus=en-2019&smoothing=3#

Google. "Google Scholar 'Developing New Perspectives on Race.'" Google Scholar. Accessed January 3, 2022. https://scholar.google.com/scholar?start=0&q=%22Developing+New+Perspectives+on+Race%22&hl=en&as_sdt=0.

Google. "Google Scholar 'Whte Awareness.'" Google Scholar. Accessed January 3, 2022. https://scholar.google.com/scholar?cites=1890401792816096393&as_sdt=5.

Gray, Vernard R. "Hell Yes We Are Going to Lybia! A Declaration to Africa and the World." Kwame Ture Dinner, November 5, 1998. http://interchange.org/KwameTure/ture111598.html.

Gurnah, Ahmed. "The Politics of Racism Awareness Training." *Critical Social Policy* 4, no. 11 (September 1984): 6–20. https://doi.org/10.1177/026101838400401102.

Harding, John. Review of the book *Training in Community Relations*, by Ronald Lippit. *Journal of Abnormal and Social Psychology* 45, no. 4 (1950): 782–783. https://psycnet.apa.org/doi/10.1037/h0049426.

Hauser, Christine. "Merriam-Webster Revises 'Racism' Entry After Missouri Woman Asks for Changes." *New York Times*, June 10, 2020. https://www.nytimes.com/2020/06/10/us/merriam-webster-racism-definition.html.

Hayek, Friedrich A. "The Atavism of Social Justice." In *New Studies in Philosophy, Politics, Economics, and the History of Ideas*, 57-68. University of Chicago Press, 1978.

Hirsch, Jerrold I. "A History of the NTL Institute for Applied Behavioral Science, 1947–1986." Boston University School of Education, 1986.

Hitchcock, Jeff, and Charley Flint. "Decentering Whiteness: 2015 Edition." Roselle,

NJ: Center for the Study of White American Culture, Inc., 2015. https://www.euroamerican.org/public/decenteringwhiteness.pdf.

Hoffman, Peter. *The History of the German Resistance: 1933–1945.* McGill-Queens University Press, 1996.

Hough, Joseph C., Jr. "Letter to Robert Terry on the July 23, 1969." School of Theology, Claremont University, CA, 1969.

Hough, Joseph C., Jr. "The Christian, Violence and Social Change," *Perspective,* X (Spring 1969), 65–85.

House Committee on Armed Forces. *Inquiry into the Disturbances at Marine Corps Base, Camp Lejeune, N.C., on July 20, 1969.* Washington, DC: Congress, 1969. http://aavw.org/served/racetensions_riots_abstract03_full.html.

Hurwitz, Alan, and Valerie Snook. "Pilot Study: Unit on White Racism." Michigan-Ohio Regional Educational Lab, June 30, 1969, https://eric.ed.gov/?id=ED034837.

Hutton, Ronald. "Writing the History of Witchcraft: A Personal View." *Pomegranate: The International Journal of Pagan Studies* 12, no. 2 (June 5, 2011). https://doi.org/10.1558/pome.v12i2.239.

InfluenceWatch. "National Education Association (NEA)." InfluenceWatch.org. Capital Research Center. https://www.influencewatch.org/labor-union/national-education-association-nea/.

'ISMS: A Dictionary of Words Ending in -ISM, -OLOGY and -PHOBIA with Some Similar Terms Arranged in Subject Order. Sheffield: City Libraries, Libraries of Arts Committee, 1963.

Isgar, Tom, and Susan Isgar. *Racism and Higher Education.* Washington, DC: United States National Student Association, 1969.

Jones, James M. *Prejudice and Racism.* Addison-Wesley, 1972. https://archive.org/details/prejudiceracism00jone.

Joyce, Frank H. "An Analysis of American Racism." Radical Student Union, 1969.

Joyce, Frank. "It's Time to Change the Water in the Fish Tank." In *A New Insurgency: The Port Huron Statement and Its Times,* edited by Howard Brick and Gregory Parker. University of Michigan Publishing, 1970. http://quod.lib.umich.edu/m/maize/13545967.0001.001.

Joyce, Frank. "White Men Must Be Stopped: The Very Future of Mankind Depends on It." Salon, December 24, 2015. https://www.salon.com/2015/12/22/white_men_must_be_stopped_the_very_future_of_the_planet_depends_on_it_partner/?utm_source=twitter.

Judicial Watch. "Judicial Watch Obtains Pentagon Anti-Bias Training Materials," July 16, 2020. https://www.judicialwatch.org/pentagon-materials/.

Judkis, Maura. "Anti-Racism Trainers Were Ready for This Moment. Is Everyone

Else?" *Washington Post*, July 8, 2020. https://www.washingtonpost.com/lifestyle/style/anti-racism-trainers-were-ready-for-this-moment-is-everyone-else/2020/07/07/df2d39ea-b582-11ea-a510-55bf26485c93_story.html.

Kaleel Jamison Consulting Group. "Judith H. Katz." https://kjcg.com/judith-h-katz.

Katz, Judith. "A System Handbook of Exercises for the Re-Education of White People with Respect to Racist Attitudes and Behaviors." EdD diss., University of Massachusetts, 1975.

Katz, Judith. *White Awareness: Handbook for Anti-Racism Training.* University of Oklahoma Press, December 15, 1978.

Katz, Judy H., and Allen Ivey. "White Awareness: The Frontier of Racism Awareness Training." *The Personnel and Guidance Journal* 55, no. 8 (April 1977): 485–89. https://doi.org/10.1002/j.2164-4918.1977.tb04332.x.

Kaufman, Michael T. "Stokely Carmichael, Rights Leader Who Coined 'Black Power,' Dies at 57." *New York Times*, November 16, 1998. https://www.nytimes.com/1998/11/16/us/stokely-carmichael-rights-leader-who-coined-black-power-dies-at-57.html.

Kelly, Robin D. G., and Betsy Esch. *Black Like Mao: Red China and Black Liberation.* Columbia University, 1999.

Kendi, Ibram X. "Ibram X. Kendi Defines What It Means to Be an Antiracist." Extract from *How to Be an Antiracist*, by Ibram X. Kendi. New York: Penguin Random House, 2020. https://www.penguin.co.uk/articles/2020/june/ibram-x-kendi-definition-of-antiracist/.

Kettering University. "1919 to 2019: The Evolution of Kettering University." May 8, 2019. https://www.kettering.edu/news/1919-2019-evolution-kettering-university.

King, Martin Luther. *Where Do We Go from Here: Chaos or Community?* Simul Press, 1968.

Klein, Joseph (Jake). "Far-left racism in government is nothing new; the military taught it for years with DRRI." *Washington Times*, September 16, 2020. https://www.washingtontimes.com/news/2020/sep/16/far-left-racism-in-government-is-nothing-new-the-m/.

Klein, Joseph (Jake). *Oppression Can't Be Measured by Outcome.* Capital Research Center, November 18, 2018. https://youtu.be/fjnCryuNOF0.

Klein, Joseph (Jake). *How Can I Be a Good Ally in the Fight for Social Justice?* Capital Research Center, August 10, 2020. https://youtu.be/hp_MMolvPwo.

Kresnak, Jack. *Hope for the City.* Detroit, MI: Cass Community Publishing House, 2015.

Lai, Kawai. Letter to attendees of Facilitating Courageous Conversations Visually seminar. "NAIS PoCC Seminar | Part 2 Recording + Other Things." Email, December 1, 2021.

Lakin, Martin. "Some Ethical Issues in Sensitivity Training." *American Psychologist* 24, no. 10 (October 1969): 923–928. https://doi.org/10.1037/h0028882.

Lamb, Brian. "Life and Career of Kwame Ture," C-SPAN, April 15, 1998. https://www.c-span.org/video/?104471-1%2Flife-career-kwame-ture.

League of Revolutionary Black Workers, Spear: Voice of the League of Revolutionary Black Workers, vol., nos. 1–2." In Detroit Revolutionary Collection. Newsletters & Newspapers, Box 1 of 1, Folder 22. https://rs4.reuther.wayne.edu/LR000874/BOX_17_PDF/LR000874_02_03_0_017_022_001.pdf.

Lindsay, James. "Stealing the Motte: Critical Social Justice and the Principle of Charity." New Discourses, May 7, 2020. https://newdiscourses.com/2020/05/stealing-motte-critical-social-justice-principle-charity/.

Lindsay, James. "The Complex Relationship Between Marxism and Wokeness." New Discourses, July 28, 2020. https://newdiscourses.com/2020/07/complex-relationship-between-marxism-wokeness/.

Longhurst, Brian. *Karl Mannheim and the Contemporary Sociology of Knowledge*. New York: St Martins Press, 1989.

Mann, E. K. "Sensitivity Training: Should We Use It?" *Training and Development Journal* 24, no. 3 (1970).

Martin Luther King Jr. Research and Education Institute. "Carmichael, Stokely." Stanford University. https://kinginstitute.stanford.edu/encyclopedia/carmichael-stokely.

Martin, Shannon E., and Kathleen A. Hansen. *Newspapers of Record in a Digital Age: From Hot Type to Hot Link*. Westport, CT: Praeger, 1998. https://archive.org/details/newspapersofreco0000mart.

McGlone, Peggy. "African American Museum Site Removes 'Whiteness' Chart after Criticism from Trump Jr. And Conservative Media." *Washington Post*, July 17, 2020. https://www.washingtonpost.com/entertainment/museums/african-american-museum-site-removes-whiteness-chart-after-criticism-from-trump-jr-and-conservative-media/2020/07/17/4ef6e6f2-c831-11ea-8ffe-372be8d82298_story.html.

McGraw, Bill. *A Journey Into Self*. Film. Western Behavioral Sciences Institute, 1969. https://youtu.be/AP2X6huruZo.

McIntosh, Peggy. *On Privilege, Fraudulent, and Teaching as Learning: Selected Essays 1981–2019*. New York, NY: Routledge, Taylor & Francis Group, 2020.

McNatt, Glenn. "Unmasking the Meaning Behind Color in African Art." *Baltimore Sun*, October 27, 2018. https://www.baltimoresun.com/news/bs-xpm-2007-04-18-0704180243-story.html.

McWhorter, John. *Woke Racism: How a New Religion Has Betrayed Black America.* Penguin Publishing Group, 2021.

Michigan Advisory Committee to the U.S. Commission on Civil Rights. "Civil Rights and the Housing and Community Development Act of 1974." US Department of Health, Education & Welfare National Institute of Education, June 1976. https://files.eric.ed.gov/fulltext/ED178674.pdf.

Michigan Education Association. "About Us: Champions for Education." https://www.mea.org/about-us/.

Mind Tools. "Force Field Analysis: Analyzing the Pressures For and Against Change." July 8, 2018.

Murray, James A.H., et al. eds. *The Oxford English Dictionary Being A Corrected Re-Issue with an Introduction, Supplement, and Bibliography.* Clarendon Press, 1933.

National Education Association. *Education & Racism: An Action Manual.* Washington, DC: National Education Association, 1973.

National Museum of African American History & Culture. "Whiteness." Archive.org, May 31, 2020. https://web.archive.org/web/20200603163659/https:/nmaahc.si.edu/learn/talking-about-race/topics/whiteness.

National Museum of African American History & Culture. "Whiteness." Accessed January 3, 2022. https://nmaahc.si.edu/learn/talking-about-race/topics/whiteness.

NBC. "Watch the Tonight Show Starring Jimmy Fallon Interview: Dr. Robin DiAngelo Wants White People to Stop Saying They're Not Racist." NBC.com, June 18, 2020. https://www.nbc.com/the-tonight-show/video/dr-robin-diangelo-wants-white-people-to-stop-saying-theyre-not-racist/4186081.

New Detroit. "A New Detroit Assessment." Supplement to the Michigan Chronicle, 1969.

New Discourses. "Authentic." New Discourses, July 8, 2020. https://newdiscourses.com/tftw-authentic/.

New Discourses. "False Consciousness." New Discourses, September 23, 2020. https://newdiscourses.com/tftw-false-consciousness/.

New Merriam-Webster Pocket Dictionary. Montréal: Pocket Books of Canada, 1964.

New Perspectives on Race. "New Perspectives on Race, New Detroit, Inc. Proposed Project Plan." Detroit, MI: Walter P. Reuther Library, New Detroit, Inc. Records UR000660, Box 107, Folder 17, May 30, 1972.

New Perspectives on Race. "What Is New Perspectives on Race?," 1973.

New York Times. "Combined Print & E-Book Nonfiction - Best Sellers." *New York Times*, February 7, 2021. https://www.nytimes.com/books/best-sellers/2021/02/07/combined-print-and-e-book-nonfiction/.

New York Times. "Paperback Nonfiction Books - Best Sellers." *New York Times*, September 12, 2021. https://www.nytimes.com/books/best-sellers/2021/09/12/paperback-nonfiction/.

New York Times. "The New York Times Best Sellers." *New York Times*, June 21, 2020. https://www.nytimes.com/books/best-sellers/2020/06/21/.

Nielsen, Kristy. "The Heat Is On." Blogger, November 23, 2009. https://kristynielsen.blogspot.com/.

Novak, Matt. "The Man Who Fought the Synanon Cult and Won." Gizmodo, September 27, 2014. https://gizmodo.com/the-man-who-fought-cults-and-won-1634267961

Novak, Matt. "Synanon's Sober Utopia: How a Drug Rehab Program Became a Violent Cult." Gizmodo, April 15, 2014. https://gizmodo.com/synanons-sober-utopia-how-a-drug-rehab-program-became-1562665776

NTL Institute. "Responding to President Trump's Memo on Diversity Training." September 21, 2020. https://www.ntl.org/about-us/actions-for-social-justice/2020-09-21-responding-to-president-trumps-memo-on-diversity-training-from-the-ntl-social-justice-hub/.

NTL Institute. "Responding to Systemic Racism." June 22, 2020. https://www.ntl.org/about-us/actions-for-social-justice/2020-06-22-responding-to-systemic-racism-from-the-ntl-social-justice-hub/.

NTL Institute. "What is Sensitivity Training?" NTL Institute. April, 1968.

Obituary Department. "Delmo Della-Dora (1926–2015)." *East Bay Times*, January 15, 2016. https://www.legacy.com/obituaries/eastbaytimes/obituary.aspx?pid=177276190.

OnlyBlackGirl. "Your Dictionary Definition of Racism Is Outdated Trash." April 13, 2017. https://medium.com/@OnlyBlackGirl/your-dictionary-definition-of-racism-is-outdated-trash-66363903d9a6.

Ordiorne, George S. "The Trouble with Sensitivity Training." *Training Directors Journal*, October 1963.

Oxford English Dictionary. "Discover the Story of English: More Than 600,000 Words, over a Thousand Years." https://www.oed.com/view/Entry/157084#eid27239959.

Parks, Gordon. "'I Was A Zombie Back Then—Like All Muslims I Was Hypnotized.'" Life 58, no. 9, May 5, 1965. https://books.google.com/books?id=KkEEAAAAMBAJ&pg=PA28

PBS. *1968: Do You Think a Job Is the Answer?*, 1968. https://www.freep.com/videos/entertainment/2018/03/16/1968-do-you-think-job-answer/32991945/.

Pilgrim, David. "The Tom Caricature." Jim Crow Museum, Ferris State University.

December 2000. https://www.ferris.edu/HTMLS/news/jimcrow/tom/homepage.htm.

Quince, Richard. *Synanon*. Columbia Pictures, May 5, 1965.

Rachels, James. "The Challenge of Cultural Relativism." University of Central Arkansas, 1999. http://faculty.uca.edu/rnovy/Rachels–Cultural%20Relativism.htm.

Ramsey, Franchesca. *5 Things Everyone Should Know About Racism*. MTV Impact, August 12, 2015. https://youtu.be/8eTWZ80z9EE.

Random House Dictionary of the English Language. Random House, 1967.

Random House Dictionary of the English Language. Random House, 1968. https://archive.org/details/randomhousedictioourda/page/1088/mode/2up.

Reed, Anika, and Hannah Yasharoff. "Looking for Books about Racism? Experts Suggest These Must-Read Titles for Adults and Kids." *USA Today*, June 2, 2020. https://www.usatoday.com/story/entertainment/books/2020/06/02/books-to-learn-more-anti-racism-adults-kids/5306873002/.

Richardson, Valerie. "Architect of NYT's 1619 Project Draws Distinction Between 'Politically Black and Racially Black.'" *Washington Times*, May 22, 2020. https://www.washingtontimes.com/news/2020/may/22/nikole-hannah-jones-1619-project-draws-distinction/.

RobinDiAngelo.com. "About Me." Accessed January 3, 2022. https://www.robindiangelo.com/about-me/.

RobinDiAngelo.com. "Publications." https://www.robindiangelo.com/publications/.

Romney, Mitt. "Black Lives Matter." Twitter, June 7, 2020. https://twitter.com/MittRomney/status/1269758561720156160?s=20.

Rosario, Isabella. "This List of Books, Films and Podcasts about Racism Is a Start, Not a Panacea." NPR.org, June 6, 2020. https://www.npr.org/sections/codeswitch/2020/06/06/871023438/this-list-of-books-films-and-podcasts-about-racism-is-a-start-not-a-panacea.

Ross, Rick. "Ten Signs of a Potentially Unsafe Group/Leader." Cult Education Institute, 2014. https://www.culteducation.com/warningsigns.html.

Sander, Richard Henry, and Stuart Taylor Jr. *Mismatch: How Affirmative Action Hurts Students It's Intended to Help, and Why Universities Won't Admit It*. New York: Basic Books, 2012.

Sandomir, Richard. "Alan Hurwitz, Teacher and Activist Who Turned to Bank Heists, Dies at 79." *New York Times*, June 15, 2020. https://www.nytimes.com/2020/06/15/obituaries/alan-hurwitz-dead-coronavirus.html.

Secretary of the Army's Senior Review Panel. *The Secretary of the Army's Senior Review Panel Report on Sexual Harassment*. Vol. 1. Washington, DC: Dept. Of The Army, 1997. https://www.google.com/books/edition/The_Secretary_of_the_Army_s_Senior_Revie/qjdfkWqJp4gC?q=%2522General%2520Of-ficer%2520Race%2520Relations%2522%2520orientation%2520seminar.

Seibert, Maria Flores. Letter to eSeminar Participants. "NYSAIS: RACE TALK IS DIVIDING US! And Other Myths about Race and Racial Literacy Curriculum in K-12 Schools." Email, December 6, 2021.

Silberman, Charles E. *Crisis in Black and White.* Random House, 1966.

Sivanandan, A. "RAT and the Degradation of Black Struggle." In *Catching History on the Wing: Race, Culture and Globalisation,* 140–66. London: Pluto Press, 2008.

Society for the Psychological Study of Social Issues. SPSSI Timeline. http://www.spssitimeline.org/.

South African History Online. "Dr Kwame Nkrumah." November 8, 2018. https://www.sahistory.org.za/people/dr-kwame-nkrumah.

Southern Poverty Law Center. "Nation of Islam." Southern Poverty Law Center. Accessed October 4, 2020. https://www.splcenter.org/fighting-hate/extremist-files/group/nation-islam.

Southern Poverty Law Center. "Sam Francis." Southern Poverty Law Center. Accessed October 4, 2020. https://www.splcenter.org/fighting-hate/extremist-files/individual/sam-francis.

Steel, Piers. "Self-Efficacy and Success: Is There Any Relationship?" *Psychology Today,* November 10, 2014. https://www.psychologytoday.com/us/blog/the-procrastination-equation/201411/self-efficacy-and-success-is-there-any-relationship.

Stanford SPARQ. "To Make Change, Start with a Crowd." Stanford University. https://sparq.stanford.edu/solutions/make-change-start-crowd.

Stevens, Ruth. "Book Reveals Influence of White Philanthropy on Founding and Future of Black Studies." Princeton University, April 10, 2006. https://www.princeton.edu/news/2006/04/10/book-reveals-influence-white-philanthropy-founding-and-future-black-studies.

Stur, Heather Marie. "Kerner Commission Report." Oxford African American Studies Center, 2009. https://doi.org/10.1093/acref/9780195301731.013.45799.

Taifa, Nkechi. "Republic of New Afrika." In *The SAGE Encyclopedia of African Cultural Heritage in North America,* edited by Mwalimu J. Shujaaand and Kenya J. Shujaa. SAGE Publications, 2015.

Taylor, Jared. "Why We Fight." Review of *Why We Fight: Manifesto of the European Resistance,* by Guillaume Faye. American Renaissance, June 30, 2020. https://www.amren.com/features/2012/02/why-we-fight/.

Terry, Robert W. "Action from the Boundary: An Historical Study of Detroit Industrial Mission 1956–1970." PhD diss., University of Chicago, 1973.

Terry, Robert W. *For Whites Only*. Erdmans, 1977.

Terry, Robert W. *New Whites—Justice and Racism*. 1970.

Thomas, James A., and Peter G. Nordlie. *Race Relations and Equal Opportunity in the Army (a Resource Book for Personnel with Race Relations/Equal Opportunity Responsibility)*. McLean, VA: US Army Research Institute for the Behavioral and Social Sciences, 1973.

Tichi, Cecelia. *Civic Passions: Seven Who Launched Progressive America (and What They Teach Us)*. Chapel Hill, NC: University of North Carolina Press, 2009.

Times Staff. "The Rev. Milton Henry, 87; Civil Rights Lawyer and Black Separatist." *Los Angeles Times*, September 14, 2006. https://www.latimes.com/archives/la-xpm-2006-sep-14-me-passings14.1-story.html.

Tochluk, Shelly. "Why Pay Attention to Race." Witnessing Whiteness. Chap. 1, Workshop 1.1 November 14, 2015. http://witnessingwhiteness.com/workshop-series/chapter1workshop1-1/.

U.S. Army Center of Military History. "U.S. Army Chiefs of Staff." https://history.army.mil/faq/FAQ-CSA.htm.

U.S. Commission on Civil Rights. *Racism in America and How to Combat It*. Clearinghouse Publication, January 1970.

U.S. Congress. *Congressional Record, 90th Congress*. April 24, 1968. https://www.congress.gov/bound-congressional-record/1968/04/24/house-section

U.S. Congress. *Congressional Record, 91st Congress*. June 10, 1969. https://www.congress.gov/bound-congressional-record/1969/06/10/house-section.

U.S. National Advisory Commission on Civil Disorders. *The Kerner Report: The 1968 Report of the National Advisory Commission on Civil Disorders*. New York: Pantheon Books, 1988.

Ullman, Richard H. "Human Rights and Economic Power: The United States Versus Idi Amin." *Foreign Affairs*, April 1978. https://www.foreignaffairs.com/articles/uganda/1978-04-01/human-rights-and-economic-power-united-states-versus-idi-amin.

Umoja, Imani Na. *Tribute to Kwame Turé, 6 April 1998 in St. Louis, MO*. https://youtu.be/mtrZp9BhN58.

Vought, Russell. "Training in the Federal Government." Executive Office of the President, September 4, 2020. https://www.whitehouse.gov/wp-content/uploads/2020/09/M-20-34.pdf.

Watts, Marina. "In Smithsonian Race Guidelines, Rational Thinking and Hard Work Are White Values." *Newsweek*, July 17, 2020. https://www.newsweek.com/

smithsonian-race-guidelines-rational-thinking-hard-work-are-white-values-1518333.

Webster's New World Dictionary of the American Language. Cleveland: World Publication Company, 1966.

Webster's Seventh New Collegiate Dictionary. Springfield, Mass.: G. & C. Merriam Co, 1967.

White, Chris. "Jack Dorsey Donates $10 Million to a Group Headed by an Activist Who Wants to Make Racism Unconstitutional." Daily Caller, August 21, 2020. https://dailycaller.com/2020/08/21/twitter-jack-dorsey-antiracism-ibram-x-kendi-boston-university/.

Wilkinson, Abi. "What Is It About the Left Which Makes Anti-Semitism so Common?" *Telegraph*, March 25, 2016. https://www.telegraph.co.uk/opinion/2016/03/25/what-is-it-about-the-left-which-makes-anti-semitism-so-common/.

Williams, Monnica. "Colorblind Ideology Is a Form of Racism." *Psychology Today*, December 27, 2011. https://www.psychologytoday.com/us/blog/culturally-speaking/201112/colorblind-ideology-is-form-racism.

Wolff, Robert Paul, Barrington Moore Jr., and Herbert Marcuse. *A Critique of Pure Tolerance.* Boston: Beacon Press, 1969.

Woodson, Robert. "The Resilience of the Black American." *Wall Street Journal*, August 6, 2020, sec. Opinion. https://www.wsj.com/articles/the-resilience-of-the-black-american-11596734835.

Woodson, Robert. *Why Conservatives Have a Problem with Black Lives Matter.* Capital Research Center, July 14, 2020. https://youtu.be/RyMgQS-Hi3w.

Woodson, Robert. *What Martin Luther King REALLY Thought About Riots.* Capital Research Center, April 7, 2021. https://youtu.be/ANn8E181BpY.

Worldcat. "Developing New Perspectives on Race; an Innovative Multi-Media Social Studies Curriculum in Racism Awareness for the Secondary Level." http://www.worldcat.org/oclc/2845458

World Wide Words. "Eating Crow." https://www.worldwidewords.org/articles/eatcrow.htm.

Wuench, Julia. "First, Listen. Then, Learn: Anti-Racism Resources for White People." *Forbes*, June 7, 2020. https://www.forbes.com/sites/juliawuench/2020/06/02/first-listen-then-learn-anti-racism-resources-for-white-people/.

Yalom, Irvin D. and Morton A. Lieberman. "A Study of Encounter Group Casualties." *Archives of General Psychiatry* 25, no. 1 (July 1971).

York, Byron. "African American History Museum Removes 'Whiteness' Chart." *Washington Examiner*, July 17, 2020. https://www.washingtonexaminer.com/opinion/columnists/african-american-history-museum-removes-whiteness-chart.